This book powerfully combines biblical reflection with personal testimony. Liesel has crafted the devotional sections with real life application that will bring God's Word to life and no doubt transform the lives of many. We commend it to you.

Nicky and Sila Lee

Associate Vicar of Holy Trinity Brompton and founders of The Marriage Course

It is often said that there are no atheists in a foxhole – but soldiers in foxholes have a very real understanding of life and death. They are often surrounded by death but have a yearning for life. This book signposts the way to life – a life in the service of others, and a life in the service of Christ.

General the Lord Dannatt GCB CBE MC DL

Chief of the General Staff 2006–2009

I feel happy and privileged to commend this volume on what it means for ordinary Christians in daily life to be soldiers for Christ. Most of us want the lax disciplines of lazy discipleship, so the Pauline imagery of our being soldiers in our King's army does not sit comfortably with us. Yet it is a rich image, and one that we ignore at our spiritual peril. This series of readings will richly bless and challenge any and all readers. I certainly need the challenges myself. Let's all be taken a few steps deeper in our walk with Christ as we absorb these readings and powerful testimonies.

Michael Cassidy

Founder of African Enterprise; Honorary Chair of Lausanne Movement

FAITH ON THE FRONTLINE

PERSPECTIVES ON LIFE'S DAILY BATTLES

CWR

COMPILED BY **LIESEL PARKINSON**

Published 2014 by CWR, Waverley Abbey House, Waverley Lane, Farnham, Surrey GU9 8EP, UK. CWR is a Registered Charity – Number 294387 and a Limited Company registered in England – Registration Number 1990308.

For a list of National Distributors visit www.cwr.org.uk/distributors

Concept development, editing, design and production by CWR
Cover image and p27: © Crown copyright 2013
Printed in the UK by Linney Print
ISBN: 978-1-78259-261-7

Acknowledgements

This book would not have been possible without the members of the Armed Forces and their families, who have contributed their stories and insights to illustrate the daily lives and issues faced by servicemen and women. The majority of their names are listed at the end of the book.

Some of the people who have contributed their stories have chosen to remain anonymous; my grateful thanks go to them too. I would also like to thank the countless people who have faithfully prayed for me, especially towards the end when time was short and the pressure was on. I fully recognise that this book would not have been written at all without God's empowering grace and presence. Thank you for praying it in! I would also like to thank CWR for their incredible support and their encouragement to write this book and its prequel, *Coffee with God*. I know that many military folk have been blessed by the generous gift of numerous free copies which CWR donated to the Military Chaplaincies of all three Armed Services. I would also like to thank the AFCU staff and various members who have given me so much support to finish this project. Particular thanks go to Val, Natalie, Julie, Fiona, Helen, Hayley and Sian. Finally, there are two people who have generously given numerous hours of their time in proof reading and creative input: Vicky Roberts, and my husband, Rhett Parkinson. Between them they have amassed over forty years of military experience and have brought richness and reality to the writing. Thank you both so much for your unstinting support and oversight of this book.

Liesel Parkinson

Foreword

The famed Victorian Baptist preacher, C.H. Spurgeon, described the Christian life thus: 'We ought to regard the Christian Church, not as a luxurious hostelry where Christian gentlemen may each one dwell at his ease in his own inn, but as a barracks in which soldiers are gathered together to be drilled and trained for war.'[1] The Christian life is certainly no picnic. We all face battles from without and within and often we are weary and wounded. The world, the flesh and devil take no prisoners.

No wonder the Apostle Paul often employed military metaphors to speak of the Christian life, summoning Timothy to 'fight the battle well' (1 Tim. 1:18). The King James Version is somewhat more robust and I think accurate in translation to the original Greek: 'war a good warfare.' Whereas a fight could suggest a one-off contest, Paul's choice of the Greek term *strateian* actually refers to a sustained military campaign. The trials of the Christian life are more than mere occasional skirmishes.

In *Faith on the Frontline*, Liesel Parkinson and friends – most of whom have served Christ in an Armed Forces context – gift us with 100 inspirational meditations built on personal testimonies of faith under fire, of courage in conflict, of experiencing God's grace in the darkest places. In Bunyan's classic, *The Pilgrim's Progress*, the warrior Valiant-For-Truth, having fought the good fight of the faith, goes to God; his last words:

> *My sword I give to him that shall succeed me in my pilgrimage, and my courage and skill to him that can get it. My marks and scars I carry with me, to be a witness for me that I have fought His battles who will now be my rewarder.*[2]

Just as Valiant passed on his sword, in this wonderful set of daily Bible studies, the authors who have stood for Christ and experienced Christ standing with them, pass on their swords to us. All who read this book will be strengthened and steadied, equipped and encouraged to fight the good fight of faith.

Rev. Simon Ponsonby – Pastor of Theology, St Aldates Oxford

Introduction

Several years ago, in that place between sleep and wakefulness, I had a vivid dream. I was standing in what I knew was the 'no man's land' of a First World War battlefield. I was surrounded by mud, trenches, barbed wire and the detritus of great battles. My ears were full of the noise of the guns, and the air was full of smoke. As I stood and looked around, I saw a figure stumble towards me out of the haze, dressed in the uniform of a First World War soldier; helmetless and bleeding. I was shocked; this was not the unknown face of a long-dead solider, it was a woman I recognised from my church's women's group. She was completely disorientated, and didn't really even seem to realise she was a soldier in a war. As I looked around, I saw many others. The trenches were full of weapons but no one seemed to know how to use them. As a result, they were completely vulnerable to the attacks of a ruthless enemy. In the confusion of that dream, I clearly heard God tell me that His Church needed to wake up and understand its role in the surrounding battle. In part, this book is my response to that call.

Many people feel uncomfortable with the concept that Christians are spiritual soldiers, and therefore by inference, the Church is an army. Perhaps this is because so many earthly wars have been fought in the name of Christianity. I am grieved by this abuse, as the Bible makes it so clear that our battle is not against 'flesh and blood' and our leader, Jesus, commands that we respond to our human enemies with love, not hate.

Our modern understanding of what Church is, and the role of individual Christians within it, has changed greatly over time. We have lost, or perhaps it would be more accurate to say that we have discarded, any military connotations. Yet, this is not necessarily biblical. William Barclay demonstrates this in his exposition of the original meaning of the word *ecclesia*, which we have translated as *church*. *Ecclesia* was not a new word when Jesus used it in Matthew 16:18, rather it was a common well-known name for which a new usage was applied. The original meaning was then a clue to illustrate a new spiritual truth. An *ecclesia* originally was the name for

> *'a convened assembly of all the citizens of a city [and] directed the policy of the city. It declared wars, made peace, contracted treaties and arranged alliances. It elected generals and other military officers. It assigned troops to different campaigns and dispatched*

them from the city. It was ultimately responsible for the conduct for all military operations ... Its two great watchwords were "equality" and "freedom". It was an assembly where everyone had an equal right and an equal duty to take part.'[1]

It is against this background that the 'Church' was called into being. It seems clear from this description, that when Jesus used the word *ecclesia* as the name for an organisation of Christ-followers that He implicitly saw it playing a part in a divine conflict.

This means that when we talk about being soldiers for Christ, we are talking about taking our place in a great spiritual battle – a war that is not ours but God's. Let us be clear, God is not engaged with a near-peer enemy armed with the same capability. No, Ephesians 6 declares that God is **above all** other rulers, powers, dominions and authorities; that includes Satan and his devilish kingdom. However, Satan is still actively engaged in open war and rebellion against God and all His agents; that includes us too, as believers in Christ. In fact, many Christians say that their real battles only began after they had committed their lives to Christ!

Paul tells Timothy to, 'fight the battle well, holding on to faith and a good conscience' (1 Tim. 1:18–19). Our spiritual battles are usually won or lost in our minds as we wage war against sin, temptation and obsession. Nicky Gumbel writes,

'We also fight with the global evils of terrorism, AIDS, starvation, poverty, the destruction of the environment and corrupt governments, as well as countless other domestic, local and international issues. In all these things there is a battle to win the victory. The Bible is realistic about this struggle. In the Old Testament, we read about physical battles against the forces of evil. In the New Testament, the struggle is more often described as a spiritual battle.'[2]

What better way to equip ourselves for this spiritual fight, than to arm ourselves first with God's instruction manual (the Bible), then to see how Christian principles are put into action by those familiar with another frontline? This is the rationale behind *Faith on the Frontline*.

I have had many opportunities to study the military, the way they work, the way they think; first as a daughter, and then as the wife of a soldier. I grew up in Zimbabwe during the 1970s in a wartime environment. I am familiar with convoys, shortages, rationing and living with uncertainty. In fact, when my husband Rhett first joined the Army and went away on exercise, returning black, muddy and smelling of gun oil, I was transported almost instantly back to my childhood. During those years, my father rotated every six weeks; six on operations in the bush and six at home doing a 'civvy' job. He would often clean his weapon on newspaper laid on the floor in the lounge when he returned. Both these fine men have contributed some of their stories to this book. I believe that stories like theirs, and the numerous others told by members of the Armed Forces, contain valuable insights to bring alive what Scripture has to say about living our lives as 'soldiers of Christ'.

It is my prayer that, as you use this book, you will grow in your faith, and be better equipped to take your place in the fight.

Liesel Parkinson

Top: Liesel with her father

Bottom: Liesel with her husband Rhett

Note to the reader:

Some names have been changed to protect the identity of servicemen and women.

Getting the most out of this book

There are many ways in which you can use this book, but I suggest you read it with a drink in one hand and a Bible in the other. The reflections each day contain two complementary Bible passages designed to provide a scriptural basis to the topic for the day. These topics address the theme of this book, which is to illustrate how ordinary men and women can live as 'soldiers of Christ'. This is brought to life through the real-life stories of members of the Armed Forces. There are certain key themes including the importance of prayer; faith and trust; God's protection; and living out our faith in the real world. These are addressed cyclically throughout the book to bring out the difference aspects. There is a glossary at the end to translate some of the military jargon into 'civvy-speak' – should you need it.

In total there are one hundred scriptural daily reflections intersected by a selection of twenty eclectic 'Notes from the Front' – standalone pieces and extended stories designed to make you think. This means that if you read the reflections regularly from Monday to Friday, reserving a 'Note from the Front' for the weekend, you will have enough material for approximately five and a half months. For those serving this could tie in well with a six month operational deployment.

Each day concludes with either a prayer or a prompt to 'pause'. These are not intended to be complete within themselves, but a suggestion to help lead you into your own prayers or provoke more thinking about your response to a certain issue.

You could complete the reading material in less than ten minutes, but I recommend you take your time and treat it as you would if you had the opportunity to pause and enjoy time with a trusted friend!

01
WITH
Rhett Parkinson

ID

1 Peter 2:4–10; 2 Corinthians 5:16–21

But you are a chosen people, a royal priesthood, a holy nation, God's special possession, that you may declare the praises of him who called you out of darkness into his wonderful light. **1 PETER 2:9**

As a young officer cadet just starting training at Sandhurst, I was given a Chit in Lieu for an Identity Card. It was drummed into us that it had to be carried at all times; on exercise, when parading, whilst on Restriction of Privileges (when it would be inspected). Several weeks later we were each issued with our MOD 90 – our ID Cards. We quickly learnt that it was not worth losing these; several cadets being marched in front of the Company Commander and fined £50, even when they had their wallets pick-pocketed! An MOD 90 generally gave you access to MOD sites, no questions asked, a privilege I did not fully appreciate until I left the Army.

When we 'join up' to God's spiritual army we are issued with a new identity also; an identity that is based entirely in Christ. Paul puts it this way in 2 Corinthians 5:17, 'Therefore, if anyone is in Christ, the new creation has come: the old has gone, the new is here!' And that new identity is awesome, not only are we to be the 'righteousness of God' (2 Cor. 5:21) but 'a chosen people, a royal priesthood, a holy nation, God's special possession' (1 Pet. 2:9). Sadly too often, having been a Christian for many years, I can take that very much for granted and forget to marvel at the wonder of those words, thanking God for that honour. Our new identity in Christ also allows us into the previously 'out of bounds' area – the very presence of God! How priceless this new identity is; it cost Jesus His very life to purchase it for us. It is up to us to protect it and guard it, just as we would an MOD 90.

PRAYER

Father God, thank You for the new identity I have through Jesus. Help me to treasure and protect my faith and do all within my power to keep it secure in You. In Jesus' name. Amen.

Flying blind

02
WITH
Jonny Palmer

Psalm 139:1–24; Jeremiah 23:23–24

Where can I go from your Spirit? Where can I flee from your presence? If I go up to the heavens, you are there; if I make my bed in the depths, you are there. If I rise on the wings of the dawn, if I settle on the far side of the sea, even there your hand will guide me, your right hand will hold me fast. **PSALM 139:7–10**

Instrument flying is quite unlike any other flying. To simulate it, a hood is put over your helmet so that you can't see anything other than the instrumentation. You have to develop the ability to build a picture in your head of what is happening around you, using information only from the instruments and what you are told. On one of my first instrument flying lessons I had just taken off from RAF Church Fenton, with my instructor in the left-hand seat, when air traffic came on the radio and told me about another aircraft in the area. I couldn't see anything and because, at the time, I wasn't very good at building these mental pictures of the situation, I believed I was on a collision course and would hit the other aircraft in a matter of seconds. Actually we were about five miles apart and the air traffic controller, with her radar screen in front of her, knew we were completely safe, but I was totally convinced I was only seconds away from death.

So often we, too, navigate our way through life unable to see the whole picture, our fevered imaginations creating a distorted impression of reality. We struggle against fear, not able to see things from a divine perspective. God says through Jeremiah, 'Am I only a God nearby ... and not a God far away? Who can hide in secret places so that I cannot see them?' God, like the air traffic controller, has all the information about every aspect of our lives at His fingertips. There is nowhere we can go, the psalmist reminds us, that is too far away from His tender love and care. He sees the whole picture, unlike us, who see only a small part.

PRAYER

Lord, help me to trust You and in Your directions for my life. Amen.

03
Anon

Stand to!

1 John 3:18–24; Matthew 21:18–22

If you believe, you will receive whatever you ask for in prayer. **MATTHEW 21:22**

My squadron was in Iraq in the summer of 2007. I was getting onto a transport plane with sixty-eight others at Basra. At this point the Holy Spirit punched me in the stomach with the urgent command, '**Pray!**' So I walked up the whole fuselage to a seat at the far end and started praying loudly in tongues with the authority of Almighty God to annihilate whatever the powers of darkness had planned for us. An hour later, as we touched down at a remote northern desert strip, there was a series of very loud explosions and the plane veered off sharply to the left. A wing of the plane had been torn off and the side of the fuselage was on fire. We had been ambushed! The runway had been lined with explosive devises. My immediate concern was that the plane would blow up, or that we would be attacked with machine gun fire. Miraculously, the plane did not blow up, and all sixty-nine of us escaped without casualties.

The original directive given to Adam by God, was to cultivate and care for the garden He had created (Gen. 2:15). The original Hebrew word translated here as 'care' carries the sense of to keep something safe, in the way that a guard or watchman would have the responsibility and authority to protect and guard something of value. No doubt Adam was equipped by God to carry out that role in the garden of Eden, although as we know, he sadly failed to keep the serpent out. Christ, called our second Adam (1 Cor. 15:45–47), has restored the mandate, meaning that through Him Christians have a responsibility to 'keep guard' of the things God has blessed us with. Jesus frequently spoke of the free access Christians have to the power that is released when we pray. John picks up this theme in 1 John 5:14, 'the confidence we have in approaching God: that if we ask anything according to his will, he hears us'. *Anything we ask!* That is when we believe in Jesus and are motivated by His love for those around us.

PAUSE

What urgent command is the Holy Spirit giving you today to pray for? What are you waiting for?

Job done

04
WITH
Phil Exner

John 3:1–21; Ephesians 2:1–10

For God so loved the world that he gave his one and only Son, that whoever believes in him shall not perish but have eternal life. **JOHN 3:16**

I was in the US Marine Corps for about thirty years. Midway through my career, I was at the home of a friend, a Coast Guard helicopter pilot. I was complaining that I hadn't had a chance to shoot at anyone yet, after all that is what Marines like to do! In fact I would have been content if I had been shot at. My friend patiently listened, with a half-smile, as I complained about my lack of fulfilment, and then he walked off. Once he'd gone I noticed that behind where he'd been standing, were some little plaques on the wall. I went over and started reading them. One of them was an award for rescuing six people from an over-turned yacht in a hurricane; another was for saving thirty British sailors from a sinking freighter. There were about half a dozen of these and I became increasingly depressed as I read each one and saw all the neat things he'd been able to do and I hadn't. My friend saw me and came over. 'Phil,' he said, 'how many lives do you have to save, before you realise that your career isn't a complete waste?' After a moment I answered, 'Well, just one I guess.'

Since then I have often thought a similar question about our lives. How many people's lives do you have to save for eternity in order for your life here on earth to have significance? In fact the way God works, it is the work of the Holy Spirit anyway. Paul writes: 'For it is by grace you have been saved, through faith – and this is not from yourselves, it is the gift of God' (Eph. 2:8). Just to be part of that process of bringing somebody to Christ is in itself a tremendous blessing that is really worth more than physically saving all the lives in the world.

PRAYER

Lord, thank You that You have called me to be part of Your rescue mission for a sinking world. Amen.

05
WITH
Rhett Parkinson

Gongs

2 Timothy 4:1–8; 1 Samuel 26:1–25

I have fought the good fight, I have finished the race, I have kept the faith. **2 TIMOTHY 4:7**

On my return from Afghanistan, I recently had to send my medals off for remounting to add the Operational Service Medal for Afghanistan, the Accumulated Campaign Service Medal and the Queen's Diamond Jubilee Medal. That brings my total to a modest eight from my twenty years of service; small fry compared to many in today's Army. I remember in training however, there was an ex-corporal who had four. At a time when most senior officers only had one or two, this was considered a good haul, so much so his nickname was 'Medals Meadowcroft'!

The concept of the Lord handing out rewards can make many of us feel uncomfortable as we know that we cannot earn our salvation, rather it is a free gift of grace (Eph. 2:8). However, towards the end of Paul's life he looks back, saying 'I have fought the good fight' and, like all soldiers, he looks forward to the 'medal parade', the official recognition for a job well done. Mixing the metaphors, Paul likens this recognition to the crown worn by triumphant athletes, a 'crown of righteousness' (2 Tim. 4:8) which the Lord, 'the righteous Judge', will hand out. This isn't something special for people like Paul, but to 'all who have longed for his appearing'. David reinforces this saying to King Saul, 'The Lord rewards everyone for their righteousness and faithfulness' (1 Sam. 26:23). Saul had made numerous attempts to take David's life. David could have taken his revenge, but chose not to, knowing that one day he would have to give an account of how he had spent his life to God. The heavenly 'medal parade' is for all soldiers of Christ. It is not a ticket for eternal life, or a way of singling some people out for special favour, but a recognition by God of the reality of the battles all followers of Jesus will have fought during their time on earth.

PRAYER

Lord, thank You that as I obediently follow You, I can look forward to hearing You say: 'Well done, good and faithful servant.' Please keep me focused on that when temptations come. Amen.

NOTES FROM THE FRONT

01 Mayday

JONNY PALMER

'Mayday Mayday Mayday, this is ISAF 30 GB Mayday. Our malfunction has grown worse and we may have to shut down all four engines in the next five minutes.'

I am not quite sad enough to rate my favourite radio calls but that was one that I will still be telling my grandkids and great-grandkids about until the day I die. It was one of the busiest pieces of airspace in the world, where they don't even wait for you to taxi off before they clear someone to land behind you, and no one said a single word for about forty-five seconds!

We were coming out of Kandahar airbase, Afghanistan, in the early afternoon and it was hot. Really hot. Shortly after take-off the captain noticed our number two and three engines were overheating and, going through the drill, we realised that we may have to shut them down. At that altitude and temperature the remaining engines didn't even give us enough performance to turn back towards the airfield, and our options were to keep the engines running until they caught fire or to crash land in the Red Desert away from known Taliban-held areas. In reality though we knew that to crash straight ahead into 100-foot tall sand dunes would mean almost certain death. So without hesitation the captain pulled the aircraft round back towards the airfield whilst we still had all four engines, thus risking multiple engine fires for the sake of getting to the safety of the ISAF-controlled base area.

Jonny in the cockpit

The extra strain resulting from the turn and increase in speed subsequently overheated engines one and four and we found ourselves in pretty much the worst position you would ever want to be in, in a four-engined tube in the sky.

After I put out my Mayday call though, things quickly looked a lot better. The weapons range between us and the runway was immediately closed and we were cleared to land on the downwind runway. With only a few hundred feet till touchdown, warnings started blaring telling us we had to shutdown engines two and three ... if we had waited any longer to decide to make that 180-degree turn to safety, I may well not be here now.

I wonder, are you chugging away quite happily in your life towards the desert? I can tell you it's not a very nice place to be and crash landing there isn't a viable option. Make a turn back and put out your Mayday. It's a risky manoeuvre, your friends and family might not like it, but it's the only way to be truly safe. I can guarantee that because of what Christ has done for you on the cross, you will be cleared for landing.

Muscle memory

06
WITH
Ben Campbell Colquhoun

Hebrews 12:4–12; 1 Corinthians 13:1–13

No discipline seems pleasant at the time, but painful. Later on, however, it produces a harvest of righteousness and peace for those who have been trained by it. **HEBREWS 12:11**

Military training frequently refers to 'muscle memory', which is the process of performing a drill, time and time again, so that it becomes second nature. In combat, one never knows quite what to expect and it is frequently terrifying, chaotic and disorienting. Through regular training and drilling, our reactions become second nature. So many recipients of bravery awards say that they were just doing what they had practised in training, as they fought off an enemy or dragged a wounded colleague out of danger.

The process of developing muscle memory is not always an easy one. It can involve the boredom of practice as well as the ache of muscle fatigue. It's similar, the writer of Hebrews assures us, to the process of training our spiritual muscles and responses. It requires discipline and endurance on our part. God's part, like the Regimental Sergeant Major and the physical training instructor, is to put us into situations and circumstances that enable us to extend our current abilities. You will know this is so if you have ever asked God for more patience. That prayer, it seems, is always answered by an immediate increase of situations where your patience is tested to the limit! God longs for us to develop our spiritual muscles, especially in the area of love. This love is described in the reading from 1 Corinthians, and although this passage is often read at weddings it is not exclusive to the realm of romance. Love is more than an emotion, it is the way of life God desires for all who seek to follow Him wholeheartedly. Why? Because God Himself is love (1 John 4:8). Growing in love with the Spirit's help will mean that one day, when we're in traumatic circumstances, we will automatically thank, praise and seek God's help for us and those around us.

PRAYER

Lord Jesus, show me where I am weak and need to build up my spiritual muscles. Put me on Your divine training programme to develop my muscle memory so that when the day of battle comes I am ready to play my part. Amen.

07

WITH

Kevin Shaw

Sense of humour

Acts 17:22–28; Psalm 16:1–11

he is not served by human hands, as if he needed anything. Rather, he himself gives everyone life and breath and everything else. **ACTS 17:25**

I used to stay regularly with a family in Portland and would attend the church in the navy base there. One Sunday, when a new chaplain started, we made a special effort to arrive on time. Enjoying the opportunity of being a visitor, I commented to my friends, 'It's nice just to be a visitor and not to have a duty to perform this week.' Whilst her husband parked the car, I walked in with his wife and their children. Greeting the new chaplain at the door, he looked me in the eye and asked me to read a lesson from the Bible in the service. How my friend laughed! I later asked the chaplain why he chose me; he commented that he didn't know why. He had never before asked anyone to read on the spur of the moment, but he just felt prompted by the Holy Spirit. When I explained my friend's laughter, we were both heartily encouraged that God has such a good sense of humour.

God desires that we serve Him, not because He needs people to do things for Him but because doing so brings *us* joy. He longs for us to serve Him freely, not out of a sense of compulsion or duty. I see this in a much smaller way when I give my own children a present. I don't give them gifts because I have to, but because I want to. Even at Christmas or on their birthdays I don't give them presents out of a sense of duty. My reward (if I needed one!) is the joy on their faces – it makes me content; or as the King James Version translates Psalm 16:11, when I walk in God's path of life, there is 'fullness of joy'. What are you doing today to serve God that gives you joy?

PRAYER

Lord, please help me to serve You with a light heart, knowing that as I do, there will be an outpouring of joy. Show me where my heart has become hard and I have ignored opportunities that You have given me to serve You. Amen.

Brokering a peace deal

08
WITH
Rhett Parkinson

Isaiah 9:2–7; Luke 2:1–20

In that day of peace, battle gear will no longer be issued. Never again will uniforms be bloodstained by war. All such equipment will be burned. **ISAIAH 9:5 (NLT, 1996)**

Having recently finished training, I was delighted to be deploying to Bosnia for six months with UNPROFOR (the United Nations Protection Force) in the spring of 1995. Having trained to use camouflage to break up the pattern of our bodies and vehicles, it was odd to be deploying with blue UN berets and bright white UN vehicles. In many ways the tour was frustrating as we had very restrictive Rules of Engagement, were constantly thwarted by the local warlords and, as the people of Srebrenica found out, the UN were unable to be an effective 'protection force'. A few months later UNPROFOR was replaced by IFOR (NATO's Implementation Force) with much more robust Rules of Engagement and peace was 'enforced' on the people!

In many of the recent conflicts like Bosnia, Iraq and Afghanistan, the emphasis has been on reaching a state of enough peace and stability to withdraw the foreign troops who have come in to bring order. Much good has been done, but compared to today's verse the situation has remained woefully inadequate. Isaiah promises that one day, when the Messiah comes, there will be total peace. We are waiting for Christ to return in the knowledge that He will establish a different kind of peace, a real peace where all the armies of the world will be disbanded … no longer needed … redundant. Nicky Gumbel on the Alpha course likens this period to the gap between D Day and VE Day during WW2. D Day in many ways was the decisive victory that led to the end of the war. As we live in the uncomfortable period waiting for Christ to return, let us pray for His peace where our troops are serving in difficult and dangerous locations.

PRAYER

Lord Jesus, Captain of the heavenly armies, we ask You to bring Your peace where there is war and fighting. We eagerly anticipate the day when You will come and bring an end to all fighting. Amen.

09

WITH
Ben Campbell Colquhoun

Field service

Luke 8:1–15; Ecclesiastes 9:9–12

other seed fell on good soil. It came up and yielded a crop, a hundred times more than was sown. When he said this, he called out, 'Whoever has ears to hear, let them hear.' **LUKE 8:8**

As Commanding Officer, I was blessed to have a number of Christians within the regiment. At one point one of these, a JNCO (Junior Non-Comissioned Officer), came up and said that at a CVM (Christian Vision for Men) weekend, he had felt God tell him to profess his faith to the regiment. The great thing about being CO was that within weeks we were able to engineer an opportunity, supported by the Padre, when we would have a field service before going away on a long exercise. At this service the soldier was able to speak powerfully and passionately in a way that his fellow soldiers would understand. As a super-fit, motivated and universally-respected soldier, it was clear that people really listened and engaged with his message. I think I would have struggled to give that message with the credibility and conviction that this soldier did, but God was gracious in putting me in a position where I could enable these seeds to be sown.

Today's reading from Ecclesiastes contains this phrase: 'Whatever your hand finds to do, do it with all your might' (v10). 'After all,' it says (I paraphrase), 'you don't know how long you will be able to do it for.' God has a purpose for each of us. He deliberately puts us in places where we can best serve Him. The way in which we serve Him will differ according to the gifting, calling and opportunities He gives us. Whatever it is that we are called to do, let's endeavour to do it today deliberately and with all our might, knowing that our words and actions are sowing seed into God's kingdom. In faith and with prayer we look forward to the time when we will see the mature crop through God's eyes, a hundred times bigger than the one we sowed.

PRAYER

Father God, show me how I may serve You more fully today in the place You have put me and with the people You have given me. Amen.

Water rations

10
WITH
Jack Crompton

John 7:37–39; John 4:1–42

Jesus answered, 'Everyone who drinks this water will be thirsty again, but whoever drinks the water I give them will never thirst … [it] will become … a spring of water welling up to eternal life.'
JOHN 4:13–14

Whilst I was surveying the construction of a new road in Thailand, we were working in incredible heat – about 40°C in the shade – and we were often not in the shade! It was essential that we drank plenty of water to keep us hydrated. We carried bottles of water on our belts but by the time we drank them it was like drinking hot water and not particularly refreshing. We also had an aluminium hay box, which was insulated on the inside and designed for keeping hot food warm. We filled it with ice and bottles of water so we could keep the drinks cold until the end of the day.

A Thai tradition at that time of year was to greet people by throwing water on them, as a blessing in anticipation of the rains. One afternoon on our way home we spied some local girls in the distance, with a bucket. We decided to bless them with a shower of water. Opening the hay box we filled our mugs with the iced water and threw it all over them – their faces were a picture! Startled, we realised that they lived in a remote village without electricity or running water and had probably never even seen, or heard of, ice!

In the reading today we see Jesus talking to a Samaritan woman and offering her not the lukewarm water which hardly quenches thirst, but His living water. We often forget how unusual this offer would have seemed to her and to the people who originally heard this account. At that time, Jews did not associate with Samaritans, nor did respectable men even talk with unknown women. However, Jesus' offer was and remains today to anyone, whoever we are, to come to Him and drink of the living water, so that we need never be thirsty, but that the water will become a spring of water welling up to eternal life.

PRAYER

Lord Jesus, fill me afresh with Your living water today. Amen.

NOTES FROM THE FRONT

02 Understanding the enemy

RHETT PARKINSON

I had recently arrived in 21 Engineer Regiment and taken command of my troop. We had less than two months to form up, train and then deploy with UNPROFOR to Bosnia on Op GRAPPLE 6. My newly married wife was keen to understand what I would be involved in for the next six months. I explained in detail that: in Croatia the Croats were fighting the Serbs; in Bosnia the Serbs were fighting the Croats and the Muslims; the Muslims were mostly fighting the Serbs and sometimes the Croats, but occasionally sided with the Serbs to fight the Croats; the Croats fought the Serbs but also at times the Muslims! My wife looked rather confused and asked, 'Who are you protecting? And who is the enemy?'

A proper understanding of who the enemy is and how he fights is essential for all military planning. It is not enough to know you have an enemy, you have to understand how he thinks and what he is likely to do. When I worked within the Combined Arms Staff Trainer based in Germany the first question in the *7 Question Combat Estimate* was 'What are the enemy doing and why?' The more command responsibility you have, the more you need to know about your enemy.

At Staff College, Step One of the Operational Estimate taught to all senior officers is 'Review of the Situation'. This is sometimes known as the Geo-strategic Analysis, and is completed to ensure that the whole staff have a common understanding of the background and underlying causes of the problem, and have a firm grip of all parties' political objectives. The aim in each case is to analyse the enemy at the beginning of the planning process. This then sets the context for the remainder of the plan and ultimately the execution of that plan. A failure to do this properly invariably means the enemy will surprise the commander, leading to failure and worse.

I have been surprised by how reluctant many Christians are to gain a proper understanding of who our spiritual enemy is and how he is likely to act. In my experience this has meant that they are unprotected and often defeated in surprise attacks. The Bible has much to say about the nature of our enemy as a simple study of the names he is given reveals. There are nearly forty different names given to Satan in Scripture, each one details a different facet of his nature. Among them he is called a liar, a thief and a murderer. He is known as the accuser, the god of this age and the deceiver. We are told that he 'prowls around like a roaring lion looking for someone to devour' (1 Pet. 5:8).

I think that it is only when we fully recognise this that we are likely to take our God-given responsibilities seriously; these include putting on our 'spiritual armour' daily and praying for God's protection over our communities and nations as well as for our families and ourselves. There will be times when the Holy Spirit directs us to launch an attack as well as maintain a defensive posture. This could take the form of prayers of intercession for specific groups or individuals, or engaging in prayer walks where we invoke God's blessing on the surroundings. I believe that doing these effectively are the 'basic drills and skills' of the Christian soldier. Mark's Gospel puts it this way, 'these signs will accompany those who believe: in my name they will drive out demons; they will speak in new tongues; they will pick up snakes with their hands; and when they drink deadly poison, it will not hurt them at all; they will place their hands on people who are ill, and they will get well' (Mark 16:17–18).

It is only when we understand the enemy and in whose authority we fight, that we will be truly effective as soldiers for Christ.

Serve to lead

11
WITH
Andy Smith

1 Corinthians 12:12–31; Ecclesiastes 4:9–12

Two are better than one, because they have a good return for their labour: if either of them falls down, one can help the other up. But pity anyone who falls and has no one to help them up. **ECCLESIASTES 4:9–10**

At the end of a carefully planned high-risk operation in Kosovo, I realised one of my best team commanders was missing – I hadn't heard him on the radio net and it was apparent that one of his team was speaking on his behalf. I quickly moved to his location to check the situation. When I arrived I was shocked to see the commander curled up in the back of his vehicle whimpering like a child. I must be honest, part of me felt a sense of anger that he had let his team and potentially the whole operation down in this way. But, I quickly realised that he was seriously unwell and amazingly his team had collectively risen to the task brilliantly in every way. I will never forget the way in which they protected his dignity. They discreetly moved him to the medical centre without creating a fuss; nothing derogatory was ever said about him. They genuinely loved him and cared for him as a father cares for his son.

Both the readings today talk about the concept of brotherly (or sisterly) love; the unselfish support and care of one genuine friend towards another. Paul likens the body of believers to a human body, each part having a different function. He explains that we go to more trouble to look after and make presentable the bits that are weaker, or perhaps not as presentable. If you want an example of what he means just look at the way people treat their feet – and the special measures they take to hide or decorate them, in order to improve them! I think Paul would have approved of the genuine care, honour and respect this sub-unit showed towards their team commander in his time of need. That day I learnt much about myself and realised that I had become more insensitive and hardened to the needs of my men than I supposed.

PRAYER

Father, please give me a heart of compassion for others. Amen.

12

WITH

Neville Howell

Trust me

John 14:1–14; Proverbs 3:1–8

Trust in the LORD with all your heart and lean not on your own understanding **PROVERBS 3:5**

I was the XO on one of the new South African Type 209 submarines. We were conducting some initial training in the chilly waters of Skaggerak, Norway; extremely cold for us South Africans!

One of the exercises was on the casing (upper-deck). Three of us went out clad in all the cold weather gear we had and got down onto the casing where the sea was coming over in huge blue icy walls. As the XO, I had to tie a rope to one of the other men and send him out to fasten the safety line for the rest of us. I assured him I had tied my best Boy Scout knot around his waist, looked him in the eye and said, 'OK Gary. Don't worry, I will hold onto the other end of this line in case you fall overboard. Trust me; we will pull you in as fast as we can!'

I expected him to give me a quizzical look or, at the very least to recheck my knot, but I was pleasantly surprised when all I got was a 'Roger Sir' and off he went. The whole operation went extremely well with no one being washed overboard or getting frozen. However, once everything was back to normal and I was sitting quietly (warm and dry) in the wardroom, I wondered whether I would be able to say 'Roger Lord' to God and do exactly as He asked me without questioning Him?

In Jesus' great discourse with His disciples in today's reading from John 14, Jesus says, 'Don't let your hearts be troubled. Trust in God, and trust also in me' (NLT). He urges them to trust Him implicitly, knowing that sometimes we will only attempt something outside of our comfort zone when we have absolute faith in the one who proposes the risk. This means that sometimes it is only once we cross the hurdle of deciding to trust Jesus completely that we can say 'Roger Lord' to His instructions.

PRAYER

Lord, help me to trust You with the things I find challenging. Amen.

Man up!

13
WITH
Ben Campbell Colquhoun

1 Peter 2:11–25; Matthew 10:1–8

'He himself bore our sins' in his body on the cross,
so that we might die to sins and live for righteousness;
'by his wounds you have been healed.' **1 PETER 2:24**

When I was in charge of a squadron of engineers, which was training to go to Afghanistan, one of the soldiers collapsed during a run. Initially it looked like heat stroke but there was also an underlying condition that meant his liver pretty much packed up. His family were flown out and the doctors thought it would be touch and go if he made it through the weekend. When addressing the squadron I asked them to pray for him. Then later, on a visit to see him in hospital with my Sergeant Major, a confirmed atheist, I was able to openly pray for healing over the soldier, who was still out for the count. Much to the doctors' surprise, he subsequently made a rapid recovery and was discharged within days. Having prayed for healing for different people a number of times, but never really seen those prayers answered, I don't know why God chose this time. Looking back, I also don't think that we gave sufficient thanksgiving for what I believe to have been a miracle.

Believers in today's readings are urged to live a different sort of lifestyle from those around them. This includes praying for those who are suffering, whether in body, soul or spirit. Peter, quoting from Isaiah 53, explains that the power to do these things is not of our own making; rather it comes from a place of dependence and trust in the victory that Christ won on the cross. This means that while *we* are responsible for seizing the opportunities God gives us, to pray with and for others, *He* is responsible for the actual results. Jesus challenges each of us; 'Freely you have received; freely give' (Matt. 10:8). This type of boldness in prayer is often a witness in itself of our faith in a God who cares so completely.

PRAYER

Lord, I confess that I often do not make the most of the opportunities You give me to pray for those I see suffering around me. Please help me to be bold, take the risk and just 'get on with it'. Amen.

14

WITH

P.M. Welland

Ambush right!

1 Peter 3:8–18; Luke 21:12–19

Always be prepared to give an answer to everyone who asks you to give the reason for the hope that you have. **1 PETER 3:15**

The principal function of 5th Battalion Rhodesia Regt Training Team (c.1977) was to give realistic pre-deployment training. At first light one particular morning B Company was bussed into virgin bush. I was the training sergeant on the leading vehicle. To say that the soldiers were bored and disgruntled would be an understatement! I believed that there was a need to sharpen everybody up! 'Ambush right!' I shouted, while firing off a couple rounds in that direction. The result was gratifying in as much that the lessons which we had been trying to drum in had obviously been absorbed; the lead vehicles accelerated and the troops on the back opened fire to the right. The problem now was that the imagined incident gathered a momentum all of its own. A 'Contact, Contact' signal was sent, along with a request for Police Reserve Air Wing support. Meanwhile, the convoy had stopped, de-bussed, and a sweep mounted. Somebody had 'seen' the enemy running towards the escarpment! At this point I owned up to starting a false alarm; it didn't go down very well at the Joint Operations Centre!

Peter writes about the need to be ready to explain the hope we have in Christ to those around us in today's reading. He talks about us speaking with gentleness and respect. Too often though, I have got it wrong and jumped in 'gung-ho', shouting 'ambush right!' It is perhaps not surprising that my endeavours have not gone down very well! The problem when this happens is that I become fearful of sharing my faith at all, and hang back dumb and wordless, trapped by fear of failure. Jesus tells us in the second reading not to fear encounters or even to precipitate them, but to trust in the Holy Spirit's guidance when they happen. What a relief!

PRAYER

Lord, please forgive me for the times I have relied on myself rather than waiting for Your Spirit's help. Please help me speak Your words with those I meet today. Amen.

Helicopter down

15

WITH
Andy Smith

Isaiah 53:1–12; 1 Thessalonians 5:12–18

Rejoice always, pray continually, give thanks in all circumstances; for this is God's will for you in Christ Jesus. **1 THESSALONIANS 5:16–18**

I have been close to several helicopter crashes in my career. The first was the Mull of Kintyre Chinook crash twenty years ago. The day before the crash, I was picked up by one of the Chinooks at Lisnaskea High School in Fermanagh. The patrol base landing pad was too small for the Chinook so we used the school playing field instead. We were whisked to RAF Aldergrove to board an RAF transport plane to RAF Manston, only minutes from our home base in Canterbury. We were at home and relaxing within hours of completing a long, cold and gritty tour. Then the Mull of Kintyre tragedy unfolded on the news, and I can remember reflecting on just how close we had been to that disaster. This wasn't the only time I have brushed with death in a helicopter crash. During my first tour in Iraq an Army helicopter was shot down during our hand-over/take-over week. All the crew were killed and the whole of B Company risked their lives for many hours under intense enemy fire to secure the crash site and recover the bodies and wreckage. The chapel was full that weekend in Basra airbase.

When we are close to terrible tragedies we struggle with conflicting emotions. We are relieved to be safe; yet our knowledge that others have died and that their families are bereaved, makes us feel guilty at our own feelings of thankfulness. In some ways this dilemma is at the heart of our faith, as Isaiah puts it in today's reading, Jesus 'was pierced for our transgressions, he was crushed for our iniquities; the punishment that brought us peace was on him, and by his wounds we are healed' (Isa. 53:5). His death meant our happiness, and we rejoice in our freedom and forgiveness – while still acknowledging His suffering.

PRAYER

Lord, thank You for Your death and resurrection; for Your life, willingly given for me. Please help me to learn how to give You thanks in all circumstances, while still being compassionate and praying for those who are hurting. Amen.

NOTES FROM THE FRONT

03 Divine protection

MARTIN WELLAND

One of the earliest memories I have of divine protection is as a small child. At that time we lived in Hebron, Palestine towards the end of the British Mandate, a time of great political unrest and turmoil. My stepfather, Jack, who was serving in the Palestine Police, was very much in the thick of it.

Shortly after my mother had married Jack we went down to Gaza for a weekend break. Late on the Sunday afternoon, we set out to return to Hebron. Jack was driving and my mother was sitting in the front with him, my younger sister Susie and I were in the back. As it got dark, Jack switched on the headlights, which were very bright. We hadn't gone very far when we were ambushed by Arab gunmen firing from the sandy desert scrub along either side of the road. Jack, who was wearing uniform, got out of the car, telling my mother to get into the driver's seat, turn the car round and drive back to Gaza. As my mother turned the car round Jack, standing in the full glare of the headlights, shouted in Arabic to the terrorists, telling them to lay down their weapons.

Jack [right], and family at the withdrawal of British troops at end of the Mandate in 1948

Meanwhile, my mother urgently told Susie and I to get down onto the floor in the back; I can clearly remember my sister saying: 'Mummy, I want to wee, I want to wee!' As soon as Jack got out of the car and stood in the headlights, the firing stopped; the gunmen probably thought that the car was a police armoured vehicle and that they were up against stiff opposition! Jack got back in and we drove safely back to Gaza. Years later, my parents told me that, had they been shot, Susie and I would have been murdered as well. Indeed, a few nights after that incident a couple of young policeman were ambushed as they drove along that same road; both were killed. Jack died in 1964, he was one of the bravest men I have ever known.

16

Anon

Standard Operating Procedures

2 Timothy 3:14–17; Psalm 22:1–31

All Scripture is God-breathed and is useful for teaching, rebuking, correcting and training in righteousness, so that the servant of God may be thoroughly equipped for every good work. **2 TIMOTHY 3:16–17**

Much time in the military is spent developing and practising Standard Operating Procedures (SOPs), namely well thought-through procedures to respond to emergency and crisis situations. As the Logistics Officer of a ship, I frequently walked through the ship familiarising myself with its fire-fighting and flood damage equipment, and thinking through how I would respond to different scenarios. I would then update my SOP log, confident in its accuracy, which would effectively become my first response to particular situations, when my heart might be racing and my thoughts not entirely clear. I also developed other routines, such as hanging my overalls next to my bunk at night ready to pull over my pyjamas quickly if needed. Emergencies and stressful situations seem often to come when we least expect or want them. Normally for me they would happen during the night when I was asleep, or even on two occasions when I was having a shower! Therefore, it is essential to train and prepare well for them before they occur.

What SOPs have you developed in your Christian life to adequately prepare you in a crisis? Mine include reading the Bible through each year, journaling and having a prayer diary. These regular activities help me to stay connected with God, so that when the crises happen I am already ‘up to speed’. I have also discovered like the psalmist in today’s reading from Psalm 22 that engaging in praise and worship during some of the most difficult and stressful times in my life has been a lifeline, providing a solace for my soul not found in any other activity. This has surprised me as singing hymns and speaking praise to God doesn’t come particularly naturally to me most of the time.

PAUSE

Are there areas of your life that would benefit from an overhaul of your SOPs? Make a start today by writing down three action points to help focus your mind (and prayers!).

Whiteout

17
WITH
Val Hall

Hebrews 11:1–40; John 20:24–29

Now faith is the assurance of things hoped for, the conviction of things not seen. **HEBREWS 11:1 (ESV)**

As I have my Mountain Leadership Certificate, I am frequently to be found out on the hills. One Easter I was leading a group in Snowdonia. On a cold, overcast morning we set off intending to walk one of the 3,000-foot ranges in the area. Our first target was a mountain called Pen yr Ole Wen. Having climbed a very steep section, which required some scrambling, it started snowing. Some of the group were not particularly well equipped and due to the worsening conditions, I counselled that we should return. The sensible way was to retrace our steps, but some of the group refused to climb back down the scrambling area. Unhappy to split the group, I decided we should carry on and come off the mountain by another route. We carried on while the cloud got dense, low and the snow began settling. I started praying hard as we entered whiteout conditions. I knew where we were on the map and took a compass bearing for the cairn on top of the mountain. I got some members of the group to count steps and others to walk in front so that I could line them up with the compass bearing. Eventually out of the murk, on cue, the cairn emerged. As we continued, the snow eased, the clouds lifted and finally we were able to return safely to the valley.

Hebrews 11 talks about faith being the belief that Christians have in an unseen reality. During the whiteout we had to cling to an unseen reality, stepping out blindly in faith, trusting in our map and compass. Trusting in an unseen Jesus can also be challenging. Jesus recognised this, in John 20:29 we see Him commanding a blessing on those who believe without seeing. Often it is only as we step out in faith that we begin to see the truth and realities emerging from the murk.

PRAYER

Lord, help me when I find faith difficult and cannot see clearly ahead. Help me to step out trusting in the things that are secure such as Your Word and Your past faithfulness. Amen.

18

Anon

A long 72 hours

Ephesians 1:15–23; Esther 4:12–5:3

I ... pray that you will understand the incredible greatness of God's power for us who believe him. This is the same mighty power that raised Christ from the dead and seated him in the place of honour at God's right hand in the heavenly realms. **EPHESIANS 1:18–20 (NLT)**

One of the worst mistakes a soldier can make in the battlefield is to lose his weapon. One of my men came to report that he had lost his 9mm pistol whilst conducting an operation at night in the desert. I told him that God knew where it was and that I would ask God to help him. He scowled back at me in unbelief. I sent him off with a Land Rover and driver to look for it, but it was like looking for a needle in a haystack as the desert was littered with camel dung and other debris. Three days later we were on the move. Suddenly a Fijian trooper, another believer, called out to his driver to stop. He had seen something. He got out and picked up the missing pistol. Throughout the Bible there are over thirty instances of deliverance coming on the third day. This was another one!

Today's two readings contain two of the examples of God's miraculous deliverance coming on the third day. The first tells the story of Esther, who represents her people's plight before the king, despite the fact that doing so puts her into considerable personal danger. The second reminds us of the miracle of Easter, and the magnificent resurrection of Christ. In both cases a 'happily ever after' seemed unlikely, but the power of God is unstoppable; it breaks in, triumphant and glorious! There are times in my own life when I long to see God's power to break through in unlikely and miraculous ways. At times like these I find that setting aside a period of time for concerted prayer, perhaps with fasting, is beneficial. Finding others who are prepared to stand alongside me is even more effective. These periods focus my attention away from myself and my issue and onto God, who has made 'the same mighty power that raised Christ from the dead' (Eph. 1:19–20, NLT) available to us. I have seen incredible results.

PRAYER

Lord God, I am awed that You love me so much. Thank You. Amen.

The assault course

19
WITH
Jos McCabe

Isaiah 40:27–31; Ephesians 3:14–21

Even youths will become weak and tired, and young men will fall in exhaustion. But those who trust in the L*ORD* *will find new strength. They will soar high on wings like eagles. They will run and not grow weary. They will walk and not faint.* **ISAIAH 40:30–31 (NLT)**

'Battle Fitness Training' they called it in the Marines. Some very fit and very mad people loved it, some hated it ... I fell into the latter category. I still remember sitting in my room five minutes before the run down to the assault course, with butterflies in my stomach, knowing the next hour or so would be one of pain, intense effort and perhaps failure. After six weeks of such training there was a 'pass-out' test. Failure might well mean removal from the course and a return to civilian life. The worst thing was the six-foot wall. By the time you reached it you had already tackled some obstacles and your legs were like jelly. I remember thinking several times of the words in Isaiah about wings like eagles ... I certainly needed them each time I hit that wall. Sometimes I did not get over it but when it counted I did ... or rather He provided the 'wings' in whatever form for me to do it.

In our ordinary lives we frequently face hurdles and six-foot walls where we know we lack the strength and resources to negotiate them successfully. These walls might take the form of sickness, betrayal, fear or disappointment. Faced with these barriers our knees can turn to jelly and our hearts can fail. But, we are not abandoned by God. Paul wrote to encourage the church in Ephesus, 'I pray that out of his glorious riches he may strengthen you with power through his Spirit in your inner being' (Eph. 3:16). God has the resources and riches we need to see us through the difficult times, enabling us to negotiate the obstacle courses with perseverance and endurance.

PRAYER

In prayer today bring the walls and fences you are currently facing to Almighty God, asking Him to give you His 'wings' and to strengthen you with power through His Holy Spirit, enabling you to negotiate even the toughest of life's courses.

20
WITH
Rhett Parkinson

Dining in night

Revelation 19:1–10; Luke 14:15–34

When one of those at the table with him heard this, he said to Jesus, 'Blessed is the one who will eat at the feast in the kingdom of God.' **LUKE 14:15**

During my troop commander's course, we were formally 'dined in' to the Corps of the Royal Engineers at the Headquarters' mess in Chatham. An ex-naval establishment, the building itself is imposing with large public rooms adorned with oil paintings and high-vaulted ceilings. The dining room had three long tables all beautifully laid and decorated with many items from the Corps' priceless and impressive silver collection. Add to this over 200 officers, each resplendent in scarlet mess kit, crystal glasses filled with wine and a bewildering array of silver cutlery with which to eat the exquisite food; it all made for an unforgettable evening.

Both of the passages in today's readings talk about the 'dining in night of all dining in nights', as they describe the great feast that God is preparing for us in heaven. This feast is likened to a wedding banquet, when the Church, described as the bride of Christ is finally joined to Christ, the Bridegroom. While this is a difficult concept for most red-blooded males to get their heads round, it is not difficult to believe that God wants to commemorate this incredible event with a stunning, sparkling celebration. However, as Jesus explains in the parable, many people will choose to decline the invitation, deciding instead to pursue earthly concerns. Jesus will fill those spaces with the poor, the marginalised and the unwanted. I wonder, what will you do with your invitation today? As Jesus explains, the invitation is given freely, but there is also a cost. He says, 'whoever does not carry their cross and follow me cannot be my disciple' (Luke 14:27). He encourages us to go away and count the cost first, and then jump in with both feet.

PRAYER

Lord, I recognise that following You will not always be easy, and sometimes what You ask of me will be hard. However, I want to follow You. Please give me Your strength to do so, so that one day I will be 'dined in' by You in heaven. Amen.

NOTES FROM THE FRONT

04 God is in the detail

JON BACKHOUSE

With my 'Best Before' date as a navy chaplain about a year away we started to have a casual look for jobs in a 'civvy' church. Almost immediately an unusual one caught our eye; it was a church in Naples with a military connection and it just ticked all our boxes. The only problem was that we would not be able to start until about five months after they were expecting.

I sent off for the details and an application form. Meanwhile, a call came through from my boss to say that he needed me to go off to sea at short notice, aboard HMS *Diamond* for a couple of months. So now I was applying for a job where I couldn't make the interview and couldn't start on time – not very promising! I made all this clear in my application and suggested that, if selected, I would be able to do an interview by telephone from sea, if they were happy with that.

To my astonishment I was selected for interview with the Bishop saying that he was happy to do it via Skype. Perhaps he thought we could do that at sea when, in fact, we could barely load an internet page in under a minute! As the ship was due to be at sea on the given date I again thought that the job was a goner.

'Ye of little faith' I hear you say! Not long after that the programme was changed for the ship to be in Souda Bay in Crete. So at least I was going to be able to get ashore somewhere. The question was, where? Sitting in a noisy coffee shop or bar was not exactly ideal for a job interview! And anyway my ancient laptop was going to need a bit of a refit.

A day in Chania, the nearest town, did yield the bits I needed for my laptop, but not a suitable location. So I then contacted the chaplain at the nearby US naval base who kindly agreed to get me onto the base to use their Wi-Fi.

On the appointed day I was directed to the library – and again found a very public location. With only a couple of hours to go I was getting a bit worried. So I set myself up in a slightly quieter corner and prepared for a bizarre experience doing a job interview with people wandering around me!

It was then that the librarian came to my rescue. I had explained earlier what I was doing and, unknown to me, she had then started to sort out the use of an old office, now a storage room. It had a desk, a power point and, even though I was surrounded by boxes, privacy! And the Wi-Fi was good, which meant a good connection and decent picture on Skype.

After all that worrying, God had every little detail sussed.

And, yes, I did get the job!

Promotion

21

Anon

Matthew 20:1–16; Romans 13:1–7

Let everyone be subject to the governing authorities, for there is no authority except that which God has established. The authorities that exist have been established by God. **ROMANS 13:1**

As an engineer squadron 2IC, responsible for the day-to-day running of the unit, I enjoyed considerable latitude and found the opportunities to make a real difference to 'the boys'' careers rewarding. However, on posting to G3 Ops in Headquarters Northern Ireland, a 3* HQ, I found I was the 'bottom of the pile' with very little responsibility. This rankled, especially when my immediate boss (a junior major) was only a couple of years senior to me. It seemed the only time I was trusted to be 'on duty' or to make any decisions was over holiday periods when he wanted to return to England. This was compounded when I later found out I'd missed promotion to major by one place.

Those serving will know how all-consuming the desire for promotion can become for the military. It can spark intense rivalry and competition between peers as they jostle for 'first place' and this can have a detrimental effect on family life, as it demands 'crunchy jobs' with their resultant long hours and lengthy periods away on deployment. Most damaging of all, for some of us, this desire can even become an 'idol', taking the first place in our hearts, minds and strength. The Bible offers a diametrically different view on promotion. Two things become immediately clear; promotion (even worldly promotion) is given not by man but by God (Rom. 13:1). Secondly, although the Bible upholds a work ethic encouraging each of us to work hard 'as working for the Lord' (Col. 3:23), the focus is not on exalting ourselves, but rather diligently serving God and others. Sometimes, this results in earthly promotion as seen in the lives of Daniel, Moses and David; but as Jesus summarised in the parable, earthly recognition is *not* the important thing, and often in the kingdom of God, 'the last will be first, and the first will be last' (Matt. 20:16).

PRAYER

Father God, forgive me for the times when I have become 'sucked in' by the desire to be promoted. Please help me to serve You alone, faithfully in everything I do. Amen.

22
WITH
Nigel Watts

Surrender

Zechariah 4:1–10; Luke 16:10–14

'Not by might nor by power, but by my Spirit,' says the LORD *Almighty.* **ZECHARIAH 4:6**

'We are the best army in the world. We don't surrender.' This was just one of many things that was drummed into us as we went through our basic officer training at RMAS. The other was this: the Army would train you and train you and train you, so that you were the best prepared infantier, gunner, engineer, or pilot (in my case), that you could be. This was so that come a time of war you could do what was required of you; tasks well within your own strength and as a result of the training you had received. I lived this out during my service career; fighting hard, finding ways around difficulties, not surrendering, relying on my skills and training. It was how everyone I knew around me in the Army lived.

Then I left the Army to work for a Christian charity. Within a few short months, I sensed the Lord speaking very gently but very powerfully to my heart: 'Nigel, you know that bit about not surrendering? I want you to surrender everything. Everything. Be totally surrendered to me. And you know that bit about training and doing it all in your own strength? You can't do anything in your own strength.' Just as God had spoken to Zerubbabel, He spoke to me, 'It is not by might nor by power but by my Spirit'. God was calling me to submit to His Lordship and put my trust in His strength, abilities and plans. It was a call to live in a manner that was 180 degrees in the opposite direction from that which I had been living for twenty-five years. He wanted to teach me that He is a faithful God, if only I would trust Him totally, no holds barred, with my 'everything'.

PAUSE

We cannot serve two masters (Luke 16:13). We are either for Him or we are against Him. As we step out in faith, we then will see Him move on our behalf. As you pray today ask God to show you any areas where you are trying to serve two masters; consider practically how to address this.

Comms

23
WITH
Neville Howell

1 Samuel 3:1–21; Romans 10:1–17

faith comes from hearing the message, and the message is heard through the word about Christ. **ROMANS 10:17**

Most of us will agree that prayer should be a two-way conversation. We can talk to God but we also need to listen. Sometimes though, because of busyness or a guilty conscience, my prayer life dwindles into a monologue or worse – I become completely silent. I joined the South African Submarine Service in 1998 and subsequently have often been struck by the similarities there are between the way we pray and the way a submarine operates. Basically, the submarine 'talks' to the outside world only when it wants to, or needs to. Other than that, it is quietly doing its own thing and trying to determine its own destiny. However, the submarine is expected to make communications contact with its 'home base' at regular intervals in order to get direction, guidance and instructions. The submarine's 'home base' can attempt to establish communications with its submarine but is sometimes unable to, due to it being 'dived' or not responding for some other reason. They will then keep 'calling' until answered by the submarine.

I was privileged to command one of our Type 209 submarines and it was during this period of command that it dawned on me how often I was guilty of not talking or listening to God about my own life, until I was in need and almost as a last option after I had been unsuccessful in determining my own destiny.

In the story about Samuel in today's reading we have a picture of God calling and calling until His voice was heard and recognised by Samuel. God calls each of us too, whether we are listening or not, and in fact it goes further than that, as the key verse reminds us our 'faith comes from hearing'. One of the ways we can hear is to regularly read God's Word. It also helps to stop speaking and just listen when we pray! God, like 'home base', will then give us fresh direction, guidance and other instruction.

PAUSE

In prayer today spend time listening and asking God to speak. You might find it helpful to write down anything you think God might be saying.

24

Anon

Turning the other cheek

Matthew 5:38–42; Psalm 119:41–46

May your unfailing love come to me, LORD, your salvation, according to your promise; then I can answer anyone who taunts me, for I trust in your word. **PSALM 119:41–42**

I really struggled during my training at Sandhurst as I lacked any previous military experience and background. However, I gave it my all, often returning from an exercise covered in mud, bloodied and bruised. It was therefore particularly humiliating to be standing with my mates as the platoon commander taunted some of us with various 'awards'. I invariably ended up with the GMFB award – I'll not say what that stands for, but let me assure you that it's offensive and humiliating!

In worldly terms taunts lead to anger, which can often lead to violence, or at the very least slow simmering bitterness and unforgiveness directed towards a person or organisation. The verses from Psalm 119 talk about another way of responding to those taunts. It is a way that brings freedom from the conditioned responses of hurt and anger. It does not involve denial of the words or the pain they caused, instead, both are acknowledged before God within the context of His unfailing love, care and salvation. God's presence is sought on the basis that He has promised it. This new reaction enables believers to have a freedom that would be denied to them had they reacted in a 'knee jerk manner'.

To turn the other cheek is not a weak response, but a strong one. It is the ability of an individual to control violent feelings towards another, in order that a model would instead be painted of Christ's victory through submission on the cross. At Sandhurst I was determined not to give up but had to choose to forgive, not just once but many times, and to leave any retribution to God. This was not an easy thing to do but ultimately has brought me into a place of freedom and peace that would have been denied to me had I chosen the path of anger and bitterness.

PRAYER

Father, may Your unfailing love and salvation come to me today according to the promises You have made to me in Your Word; as it is only through them that I can respond to others in a way that brings glory to Your name. Amen.

Risk

25

Anon

Luke 9:1–6; Isaiah 6:1–8

Then I heard the voice of the Lord saying, 'Whom shall I send? And who will go for us?' And I said, 'Here am I. Send me!' **ISAIAH 6:8**

When I was a young officer serving at sea, I heard that one of the ship's company had to return home on compassionate leave as his wife had miscarried her baby. This particular LMEM was one of those people who was always cheerful and would go the extra mile to help you. I wondered how I should respond as a Christian, so decided to take a risk and write a card to the couple. In it I shared a few verses of Scripture and wrote about how the Lord knew and loved their baby. I posted it to their home address. Two weeks later I was walking down the ship's drag, when I saw the husband at the other end. Filled with mild panic, I wondered what he had made of my card. Seeing me, he made a beeline to thank me for the card. He shared that it had touched him and his wife so deeply that she kept the card next to her bedside to read at those moments when comfort was especially needed. A small God-risk can make a big difference!

It is interesting that the first task Jesus sets His disciples to do 'solo', is to spread the good news about the kingdom of God through words confirmed by miraculous signs. I think we underestimate how 'risky' those first followers would have found those instructions. 'Take nothing,' says Jesus, 'rely completely on God … heal the sick and cast out a few demons'! How quickly we read and remember their excitement when they got back and gloss over the very real nervousness and fear they must have felt beforehand. God is concerned about our spiritual growth. We grow when we take kingdom risks; experimenting with possibilities which put us outside of our comfort zone into the place where we have to be totally dependent on God and not on our own ability. What 'godly risks' is God asking you to take today, and how will you respond to his 'dare'?!

PRAYER

Lord, I pray that like Isaiah I will say, 'Here I am Lord, send me.' Amen.

NOTES FROM THE FRONT

05 Landmine

MARTIN WELLAND

Martin pictured top right

B Company 5 Rhodesia Rifles, Company Headquarters based at Marymount Mission.

Good Friday April 1975 was hot and dry down on the Mozambique border to the east of Marymount Mission, where the platoon had been patrolling for the past ten days. The dust rolled up in a huge red cloud behind us as we journeyed back to Marymount. I was the lead driver in the two truck convoy. Standing orders stated that vehicles should maintain visual contact with one another but with the dust this was impossible, either for me using my side mirror or for the ten blokes on the back; for some reason radio comms were also lost.

After some time, on arriving at a fork in the road I thought it would be a good idea to pull over and wait for the others to catch up, which in due course they did about ten minutes later. Drawing up alongside, the very irate platoon commander proceeded to give me a 'thick ear' (it wasn't my fault, boss; I'm only the driver!). Anyway, in the event, the driver of the other vehicle was told to take the lead.

As I pulled over to the right to follow him there was an almighty bang directly under my seat. I remember being lifted up and my head hitting the roof of the cab hard. Fortunately I was wearing a helmet and didn't suffer any injury; nobody else was hurt, thanks I believe in large part due to standard army practice of water-filled tyres. There was a hole two to three feet deep in the road and the long veldt grass on either side was flattened for some distance. After a bit of shouting everybody de-bussed, took up an all-round defensive position and waited for the others to come back. By now it was late in the afternoon and too late for vehicles to be sent from Marymount to uplift us, and it was decided that we should base up for the night where we were. A little while later, just as it was getting dark, somebody spotted what looked like suspicious activity going on not very far from where we were. Fearing an ambush Lt Smith gave the order to open fire; this went on for a minute or so when it became apparent that there was probably nothing there! In fact in a subsequent follow-up the next morning, nothing was found.

On Easter Saturday I wrote a short letter to my wife; in it I didn't say anything about what had happened, only: 'Keep on praying, your prayers are being answered!'

26
WITH
Jack Crompton
and Vicky Roberts

The power of recall

Luke 6:46–49; James 1:16–27

Anyone who listens to the word but does not do what it says is like someone who looks at his face in a mirror and, after looking at himself, goes away and immediately forgets what he looks like. **JAMES 1:23–24**

Whilst conducting a survey task in Malaysia we were accommodated just outside of Sabah in two large flats, which the locals believed to be haunted. My friend was alone in the flat one night when he was awoken by a strange noise. On the third time of hearing it, he was determined to prove to himself that he didn't believe in ghosts and wasn't afraid. He started searching on the ground floor, working upwards, leaving the lights off as an act of bravado. Having found nothing, he decided to use the bathroom before returning to bed. As he opened the door a light came on and a face stared at him from the wall opposite! He was scared out of his wits. Only later did he realise that it was his own face that had stared back at him from the mirror! The lights in the bathroom, well known for their dodgy connections, must have completed their circuit as the door opened.

Today's reading from James talks about someone who looks in the mirror but immediately forgets what he looks like. This is a great description of how we so often act; we read the Bible but forget to put it into practice during our everyday life. We get carried away with banter and gossip and forget to watch our words. Or we lack faith and wisdom and don't even think of asking for God's help. Jesus said that anyone who heard His words but failed to put them into practice was like the man who built a house without a foundation. When the storm hit, the house was washed away. Neither of these pictures is very flattering and in order to change we need the help of our 'Father of Lights' to show us who we really are.

PRAYER

Lord, help me to be a doer, not just a hearer of Your Word. Amen.

'Blind' faith?

27
WITH
Neville Howell

Psalm 118:5–14; Proverbs 30:1–6

It is better to trust and take refuge in the Lord than to put confidence in man. **PSALM 118:8 (AMPLIFIED)**

I had often visited submarines, but it was only when I volunteered to join the South African Navy submarine squadron and sailed on board for the first time as a crew member that it dawned on me that I, along with the rest of the crew, put our lives in the hands of the people who had made and maintained the boat and all its equipment! As panic rose, I walked over to something with which I was familiar to try and calm my imagination down a bit – the sea chart – only to realise that I was relying completely on the guy who drew this chart up years ago as I had no way of seeing outside the dived submarine! We were 'flying' blind in a machine that was built by people I did not know at all and would probably never meet.

Cutting out the noise of the voices in the submarine operations room I realised how silent everything was and couldn't help but wonder if it meant everything had stopped working. Not getting any indication from observing the other people, I decided I had no choice but to trust that everything was in order. Operating in a submarine is an act of faith and trust; faith in the equipment such as the sonar, echo sounders and sea charts. And trust in the people who have produced them all.

The Bible says that although we can trust people, God is even more trustworthy, and as the key verse points out, if there is any doubt between whom we trust, God wins every time. We can take Him at His word; Proverbs 30:5 puts it like this, 'Every word of God is flawless; He is a shield to those who take refuge in Him.' That first trip was now twenty years ago and I can honestly say that my confidence in all the equipment and trust in those unseen people has never let me down. And as for God ... well, He has proved even more trustworthy!

PRAYER

Father, please help me to trust You more completely today in everything I do. Please heal any areas where I find it hard to trust others. Amen.

28

WITH

Vicky Roberts

Weapons

Ephesians 6:10–18; 1 Peter 5:7–9

Put on the full armour of God, so that you can take your stand against the devil's schemes. **EPHESIANS 6:11**

One of the disciplines expected in the Army, especially for dismounted infantry warfare, is that of memorising the characteristics of various types of weapon, both of our own and of the enemy, including their ranges, arming distances, and whether they should be employed from the side, from the front, or with any other key constraints or operating principles. Initially this was somewhat of a memory exercise for me and seemed rather pointless. However, once actually deployed on the battlefield, whether on exercise or for real, I discovered that it is the only way of knowing whether we are in range of the enemy's weapons or, hopefully, of being able to position ourselves in such a way that we can attack the enemy from our position with our own weapons, before they can reach us with theirs.

In Ephesians 6 we learn of the key spiritual armour provided to us by God, both for offensive and defensive action. There are also important lessons we can learn from Scripture about the enemy's tactics and procedures. However, the only way we will *know* our enemy's tactics is if we study the manual – God's Word! By diligently practising with these weapons of truth, righteousness, peace, faith, salvation, the Spirit and prayer, and by being aware of the enemy's behaviour, we can indeed stand firm against the devil's schemes. 1 Peter 5:8–9 also warns us to resist the devil, standing firm in the faith, not just for ourselves but for other believers. Make an effort today to be on your guard for the enemy's tactics, to put on your heavenly armour, and to pray in the Spirit on all occasions, not just for yourself but also for those around you, that they may be able to stand firm.

PRAYER

Lord of heaven's armies, help me to study Your Word in season and out of season so that when bad days come, I may stand firm. Today I want to put on the spiritual body armour You have given me, so that I can play my part in resisting the devil. Amen.

Contact RPG

29

Anon

Joshua 1:1–9; Matthew 5:1–12

Have I not commanded you? Be strong and courageous. Do not be afraid; do not be discouraged, for the LORD your God will be with you wherever you go. **JOSHUA 1:9**

Everyone has a story to tell and everyone has had a wound that needs healing. This is my story …

It is a dark night, I am tired – another operation. Our Infantry Company is heading 'home' to the relative comfort of our tents and I am looking forward to my camp cot. Then, the ambush – a Warrior hit by an IED. 'Contact RPG'. Small arms fire – tracer rounds fly through the night. Our own, dead. Soldiers so brave under fire. Medics administer aid. Helicopters land. The wounded are extracted.

The enemy withdraw and the firing stops. The sun rises, yet we still wait – there is intelligence to be gained. We leave this hell, and go back to base; a 'Well done, mate,' but blood-stained boots and smock tell the story. The de-brief, then the tears – 'Why God? Where were you?' Finally, sleep. But as the sun rises again, I think of the families, many miles away, who face that 'knock on the door', followed the news reports – the yellow stripe across the bottom of the TV screen. But, soon it is the next day and for us, back into the battle again – 'God,' I say, 'I need you now,' and ... God is still there.

God is still there ... God is not limited by space or distance. He is with us when life is sweet, but He is also with us in pain, sorrow and suffering, just as He told Joshua He would be. In fact, Jesus said in His famous Beatitudes, that when we are in pain and sorrow, He commands His special blessing. 'Blessed are those who mourn,' He says, 'for they will be comforted' (Matt 5:4). Jesus also called the Holy Spirit by another name, 'the Comforter'. The Amplified version of the Bible expands His name like this in John 14:26: 'Counselor, Helper, Intercessor, Advocate, Strengthener, Standby.'

The story you tell may not be from the frontline, but God still wants to heal your wound.

PRAYER

Lord Jesus, please send Your Comforter. I ask for healing and a revelation of Your presence in this area. Amen.

30

Anon

Ingenuity

Psalm 104:1–35; Lamentations 3:22–23

How many are your works, LORD! In wisdom you made them all. **PSALM 104:24**

I have fond memories of how we used to be creative and improvise on board ship, where space was always at a premium. This could take a number of forms. For example, the ship's bell would be used as a font for baptisms. Bible study or prayer meetings could take place in all sorts of places, ranging from someone's cabin (often smaller than your bathroom at home), to weapon machinery spaces. For those of us who liked to run, this often involved pounding round the ship's upper deck, being blown quickly up one side by the wind (depending on the ship's direction and speed), then making painful progress into the wind on the other side. Flight deck sports were always fun and certainly not for the faint hearted! This was because the balls were regularly lost over the ship's side, so we would improvise with ones made up of scrap materials and masking tape! We played a game called 'bucketball' which involved people standing on chairs holding and moving buckets (the ship's version of basketball). Perhaps one of the most unusual places where I have sunbathed is next to Harpoon long-range missiles on the upper deck.

God is the ultimate Creator and, since we are made in His image, we are meant to be creative too. What exactly that means is hard to define, though most dictionary definitions contain the idea of bringing something original, produced in the imagination, into existence. Too often we relegate the concept of being creative only to those with an arts background; however, the scientist who creates a new formula and the engineer who builds a new structure are equally creative. In fact, all God's love and mercies are characterised by constant re-creation and freshness. We even see this surprisingly in the middle of one of the saddest books in the Bible, Lamentations. Jeremiah puts it like this: God's mercies 'are new every morning; great is your faithfulness' (Lam. 3:23).

PAUSE

What opportunities in your work and leisure do you have to be creative? Thank God today and pray for more opportunities to use them to reflect His glory.

NOTES FROM THE FRONT

06 His strength and not my own

SIMON MAGGS

Before joining the Army, I decided to run a marathon. I had the physical build of a long-distance runner and was confident that I could prepare myself by sticking determinedly to a self-imposed training programme. Four months later, I had become extremely fit, running fifty miles a week on roads and absolutely hooked on the endorphin highs that go with long-distance running. As a result, I foolishly ignored all the warning signs of overtraining; I began running on the camber of the road to relieve the pain in my left leg and stuck rigidly to my training programme, despite developing acute backache, which forced me to lie down in the evenings.

One evening when I was out on yet another fifteen-mile run, I suddenly developed sharp pains in my knees, which forced me to stop running completely. Frustratingly, none of the doctors or physiotherapists that I saw were able to give a clear diagnosis of the problem and I was sent away with nothing better than ibuprofen, Tubigrip and the advice to 'stop running', which was the last thing I wanted to do. The sudden absence of endorphins and the realisation that this might be a serious injury, which could prevent me from joining the Army, brought me literally to my knees and I asked God in desperation to help me out of the mess that I had made.

Seeing that I was at my wits' end, my dad suggested that I speak to Mark, a member of our church who prayed for people. After the Sunday service, I approached this very tall, no-nonsense character, who turned out to be a police unarmed combat instructor, as well as a Christian. When I described my problem, he told me to sit down on a chair and hold out my legs in front of me. For the first time, I noticed that my left leg was a full inch longer than my right! This explained why I had been compensating by running on the camber of the road and also the knock-on effect on my back, due to the difference in leg length.

Simon on duty

Mark then took me completely by surprise by asking whether I wanted to be taller or shorter! I replied that I would like to be taller and instinctively closed my eyes before he started praying. Mark told me instead to keep my eyes open and to watch my legs closely as he was going to pray for the right one to grow out to the same length as the left! With a very simple prayer, Mark commanded my right leg to grow in the name of Jesus and (I kid you not) my right leg grew a full inch before my eyes in about five seconds. Clearly, I was amazed and delighted – I thanked Mark and went home to tell Dad, praising God. I knew from my parents that miracles were real but this was the first one I had experienced for myself!

Looking back, I realise that God used this situation to disciple me as a young Christian. All my misplaced arrogance was blown away by this sudden injury, forcing me to place my whole future into God's hands. I had to turn away from doing things my way (what the Bible calls repentance) before He was able to make something of me, but in His way. Ultimately, none of our abilities and strengths are of any use unless they are submitted to God's control.[3]

31

Anon

Pairs, Fire and Manoeuvre

Matthew 18:1–22; James 5:13–16

Again, truly I tell you that if two of you on earth agree about anything they ask for, it will be done for them by my Father in heaven. For where two or three gather in my name, there am I with them. **MATTHEW 18:19–20**

At Sandhurst one of the first things you learn is the buddy-buddy system. At its most simple it consists of a partner checking you over to make sure nothing is out of place before you step out on the parade square. Then, on exercise you share a shell-scrape and poncho to make a basher, living in a hole together! However, it is on operations, when the buddy-buddy system is of most value. In a contact situation you adopt a TTP (Tactic, Technique and Procedure) known as 'Pairs, Fire and Manoeuvre'. Turns are taken in which one person fires at the enemy, protecting the other as they carry out some vulnerable activity, like moving into a new position or changing a magazine.

In my Christian life I have experienced the huge benefits also of adopting a buddy-buddy system; a same-sex friend with whom I meet to pray regularly. We sit and chat about the week, before committing it to the Lord in some simple prayer. This is a safe place to do exactly what James instructs in his letter: confess my shortfalls and failings, my struggles with temptations and doubts, to ask for prayer for healing or boldness. We talk about the big things and the trivial. Sometimes, I give more prayer than I receive; sometimes I receive more than I give. This is a huge strength and support; but more than that, Jesus Himself, according to Matthew 18:19–20, is present with us.

PAUSE

Is there someone with whom you could meet regularly for prayer? It is important to choose carefully and it can be helpful to ask some simple questions about a potential 'buddy': are they trustworthy? Will they respect my confidence? Do they live close enough for us to meet regularly? Do they really want to follow God, or will their issues cause me to backslide? Will they be as open and transparent with me as I would like to be with them?

Joint effort

32
WITH
Andy Smith

Romans 12:9–21; Philippians 2:1–4

Do nothing out of selfish ambition or vain conceit. Rather, in humility value others above yourselves, not looking to your own interests but each of you to the interests of the others. **PHILIPPIANS 2:3–4**

As a Company Commander in Kosovo several years ago, I recall a situation where my company was tasked with simultaneously securing several dwellings in different parts of the city in order to allow special police squads to arrest a Person Indicted For War Crimes (PIFWC). The operation was complex and partly involved the securing of two high-rise flats and several stairwells. Each team had to work independently, with stealth, so as not to compromise any of the target locations. It was unclear how long the PIFWC might stay in the flat and so a decision was taken to act without rehearsals. Presence of mind, speed, aggression and agility were all necessary to achieve the desired outcome. Every team commander had critical tasks to perform in order for the whole operation to succeed. As soon as 'H' hour passed, my command team moved to its designated location to control the main target area as the military teams broke cover. The special police squads used explosive charges to gain entry to the flats and the arrest was swift and successful. Within seconds the PIFWC was bundled into a police vehicle and sped away before any sympathisers had been able to react.

The military are well known for their carefully planned and well-executed orders, and for acting as a well-disciplined team, where every member knows their duty. Sometimes these duties, in the interests of national and international safety and justice, can be unpleasant. However, as demonstrated here, good teamwork and planning minimise the danger and loss of human life. Good teamwork can be harder to achieve in Christian circles without the well-defined hierarchies and roles that exist in the Regular Army. However, the need for this unity is essential if we are to share the good news of God's kingdom with a broken world. Paul writes, 'Be devoted to one another in love. Honour one another above yourselves' (Rom. 12:10).

PAUSE

The key to unity is to prefer the other person and put them first. Bring the people you find difficult to the Lord.

33
WITH
Ben Campbell Colquhoun

Prayer power

Luke 6:27–36; John 15:18–27

But to you who are listening I say: love your enemies, do good to those who hate you, bless those who curse you, pray for those who ill-treat you. **LUKE 6:27–28**

Several years ago I was privileged to be selected for the Advanced Command and Staff Course, where the top third of majors were given further education and training. It was a fascinating time, but also a competitive one with more testosterone than Alan Sugar's boardroom! I found one colleague in particular extremely difficult as he would go out of his way to ignore, marginalise and ridicule me. This inspired me to pray for him daily. I prayed regularly for the various challenges in his life and for him to be encouraged.

Both of today's readings outline the harassment Christians can receive on account of their faith. Jesus explains that the hatred that leads to persecution comes from the world's hatred of Christ Himself. As believers who worship Christ rather than 'the spirit of the world' (1 Cor. 2:12), we are automatically 'the enemy' of the world. Some people may be more openly antagonistic towards us than others. As always it is not the people who are the real issue, but the 'spirit' that is operating behind them whether they know it or not! But rather than responding in anger or bitterness, we can choose to respond in love.

Furthermore, by praying for those who hate us, the situation can change completely as I discovered when I prayed for my difficult colleague. Over a couple of months, his attitude towards me completely changed and he in turn was positive and supportive back. God is good! Praying for others works!

PAUSE

Ask God to bring to mind those who have hurt and persecuted you over the years. As you do so, ask God to help you to choose to forgive them and give you His love for them. Then start to pray blessing for them for the various challenges they face in their lives. How easy you find this will depend on the level of hurt and anger you still carry. But as you persist it will become easier and things will change!

Washing parade

34
WITH
Val Hall

Micah 7:18–19; 1 John 1:1–10

If we claim to be without sin, we deceive ourselves and the truth is not in us. If we confess our sin, he is faithful and just and will forgive us our sins and purify us from all unrighteousness. **1 JOHN 1:8–9**

No. 2 Army Education Centre (AEC) used to be at Claro Barracks, Ripon, occupied at the time by 38 Engineer Regiment. The Centre overlooked the guardroom. Whenever possible, my husband used to give me a lift to and from the barracks during his commute to work. This meant that I was often still around in the early evening, when the miscreants identified that day had to parade after work in front of the guardroom. One evening there was the usual shouting as those on parade were marched to the guardroom just as my husband arrived to collect me. Creasing himself with laughter, he called me over to watch. Each soldier was carrying a large plastic bag in one hand and a large box of washing powder under the other arm. When they had halted outside the guardroom and had done a left turn to face the guard commander, they were ordered to hold out the bags (doubtless containing their washing) in front of them. There followed a lengthy lecture on hygiene before the squad were brought back to attention and marched off again – presumably to the laundry to make recompense for their earlier sins!

Within the military, the punishment for minor offences is often a public event, involving humiliation and incurring ridicule. How good it is instead to have a loving and forgiving Father as God, who longs to forgive and cleanse us of our sin quickly and completely, rather than a stern Sergeant Major-type God who seeks to shame and debase us in order to teach us a lesson. As Micah puts it so eloquently, 'Who is a God like you, who pardons sin and forgives the transgression of the remnant of his inheritance? You do not stay angry for ever but delight to show mercy' (Micah 7:18).

What public or secret sin is spoiling your relationship with God today?

PRAYER

Father God, I pray for Your forgiveness in these things; knowing that You are quick to forgive and hold no record of wrong. Amen.

35

Anon

Love your enemy

Matthew 5:43–48; Titus 3:1–8

But I tell you, love your enemies and pray for those who persecute you, that you may be children of your Father in heaven.

MATTHEW 5:44–45

In 2007, while on tour in Iraq, I was given orders to snatch a top insurgent leader. He had kidnapped and shot eleven Iraqis. He was known to be leaving Basra within the next twelve hours with his personal bodyguard in a convoy. With depleted resources and in desperation I cried out to God to help me.

God's response was immediate and unexpected. He made it clear that He wanted me to pray that no harm would come to this man and that I should pray for his salvation. I responded in disbelief, thinking, 'Did David have to pray for Goliath?' However, that afternoon, God changed my heart and opened the way for His divine intervention. Four SAS men were tasked to help me. As his convoy left Basra they split up into two groups. I put two of the SAS soldiers in the smaller helicopter. With both helicopters up in the air and trying to carry out a hard stop on the insurgent vehicle groups, what happened next was miraculous. The helicopter with the two SAS soldiers pursued two vehicles that had become separated from the other four. Choosing the lead vehicle, they flew so that the helicopter sat a few feet above the car – almost turning it over with the down draught. It forced the lead car to stop in a cloud of dust by disorienting the occupants. To the amazement of the two SAS soldiers, the front passenger seat door opened, and out came a man limping, with a stick, shouting abuse at the helicopter! It was our man – in his arrogance and anger he had got out of the car and identified himself. Quickly, he was bundled into the helicopter and taken to a secure place.

Paul reminds Titus that God 'saved us, not because of righteous things we had done, but because of his mercy' (Titus 3:5). He describes Jesus being the epitome of God's kindness and love. We too need to be Christlike, loving our enemies and praying for those who persecute us.

PRAYER

Lord, You know how hard I find it to love some people. Please help me. Amen.

NOTES FROM THE FRONT

07 Heavy bergen and burden

CLARE CALLANAN

A young soldier sits in front of me. His eyes flick around the room constantly, avoiding mine. His legs jig up and down to a rhythm only he knows. His hands are restless and agitated. He rolls his tongue around the piercing in it. He tells me that he does not talk much and so we wait. I reassure him that the biggest step he will ever have to take has been taken; he has stepped up and knows that he needs to talk. He has lifted off that bergen full of heavy rocks of whatever is burdening him. And now it is my turn to listen ... with integrity, with love and with the grace of God.

The young man who told me that he does not talk much pours out his story. The dam has been breached and the waters spill over. Five years ago, at the age of eighteen, he passed out from his basic training and was posted, together with a close mate from training, straight to his unit. Within a few months he found himself in Afghanistan on daily patrols in a highly kinetic part of Helmand, with a job to do. He was in the lead with the equipment that detects Improvised Explosive Devices, checking the ground with care and deliberation – the lives of the rest of the patrol at stake. His eyes look down a little more now; not so restless but they search inside for the memories. It is clear he can still smell, see, hear, taste and touch every part of the incident that blew up his training mate, the best friend he has ever had.

Seventy minutes later, I gently tell him that he has been talking for over an hour. The surprise on his face and the glance at long last into mine, reveals to me a flash of that eighteen-year-old boy who became a man within the space of one heartbeat and one IED, on a dusty Afghan path. The man who emerged from the debris of that day was burdened and bowed with grief. The screams of his mate and the thumping of the medical evacuation helicopter can never drown out the small voice of blame; the smell of explosive and the choking of dust can never overcome the taste of failure; the pictures play at night over and over.

I know his story is not unique; there are many young and older soldiers with stories like this. There always have been and sadly, there always will. But this particular one was gifted to me and is in front of me through the listening grace of an all-mighty and all-compassionate God. Over the following weeks those heavy rocks emerged from his load and we looked at them carefully and tearfully at times, and then left them to one side; not to be taken up again.

We examined the grief and guilt and blame and hopelessness; and acknowledged these emotions as we recognised the life that has in the last five years grown larger around him.

A young soldier sits in front of me now. His eyes look into mine, engaging with me. His legs rest relaxed in a sprawl, the rhythm stilled. His hands lie in his lap or carefully turn the pages of the book that is his battalion's photographic record of that operational tour; they stay briefly on the page showing the obituary of his friend ... and then move on and point out with a smile the group photograph of his platoon. He tells me that he talks more, but I already know that. He sits here because some weeks ago he came to me and Christ walked in with him, sat down as well and said, 'Come to me, all you that are weary and are carrying heavy burdens, and I will give you rest.'

36
WITH
Jos McCabe

The Chapel Spire

Titus 1:5–9; Matthew 12:33–36

An elder must be blameless, faithful to his wife, a man whose children believe and are not open to the charge of being wild and disobedient. Since an overseer manages God's household, he must be blameless – not overbearing, not quick-tempered, not given to drunkenness, not violent, not pursuing dishonest gain. Rather, he must be hospitable, one who loves what is good, who is self-controlled, upright, holy and disciplined. **TITUS 1:6–8**

Fermanagh, Northern Ireland, 1979. A troop of Royal Marines was based in the recently bombed RUC station of Kinawley. The Company Commander told the main gate Sanger guards he wanted to test the procedures on how to deal with a flatbed vehicle about to fire mortars into the base. 'For exercise for exercise,' the tannoy blared, 'flatbed truck with mortar in the lane beside the station, mortar drills to be followed.'

The marines reacted immediately; the 84mm team were to fire a TPT round into the truck to dislodge it. The team, who had not heard it was an exercise, fetched the 84mm and ran to the gate to be met by the Company Commander. 'Follow me!' he said and they ran to the lane. No truck. The team looked at each other, 'What do we do sir?' 'Carry on men,' he said as he began to walk back towards the station. The team promptly loaded and fired. The round hit a road sign, ricocheted and knocked the spire off the neighbouring Roman Catholic church! Whoops, not good for community relations! An enquiry exonerated the 84mm team and the Company Commander learned a very important lesson that day in communication and obedience!

Everyone knows that people will copy the example their leaders set them. That is why Paul sets the bar so high for those in leadership within the Christian Church. An undisciplined follower often highlights the leader's own disorderly thinking. Someone has quipped that 'Christians are the only Bibles that most people will read.' Whether we like it or not our words and actions will influence others, especially if we are involved in leadership, as they are the 'overflow' from our hearts. (Matt. 12:34, Amplified).

PAUSE

Get right with God first and foremost today so that you can be the example to others you are called to be.

Hurry up ... and wait!

37
WITH
Rhett Parkinson

Proverbs 16:1–3,31–32; Galatians 5:13–26

Grey hair is a crown of splendour; it is attained in the way of righteousness. Better a patient person than a warrior, one with self-control than one who takes a city. **PROVERBS 16:31–32**

On one of my first exercises as an engineer troop commander, I found myself sitting in my vehicle in the early hours of the morning. I'd sent numerous reports in about the progress of the bridge my troop were constructing up to squadron headquarters. Feeling jaded, I decided to wander the one hundred or so metres down to the bridging site and see how the boys were getting on. It was dark and the boys were coming to the end of a four-hour build. As I walked about, I saw a roll of Class 70 trackway laid out and ready to unroll down the slight incline. Bored and keen to get the job done I gave the roll a good kick and was rewarded by a roar as it unwound ... narrowly missing a couple of my sappers! Whilst my staff sergeant calmed the irate corporal in charge of the task, I beat a hasty retreat to the safety of my vehicle. Not one of prouder moments!

The Bible has a lot to say about the need for soldiers of Christ to surrender themselves completely to God, which includes the ability to wait patiently; something that most of us struggle with! Paul describes it like this, 'the flesh desires what is contrary to the Spirit, and the Spirit what is contrary to the flesh. They are in conflict with each other' (Gal. 5:17). To God, patience and self-control are more desirable than military expertise. Humanly speaking they are qualities that can take a lifetime to acquire (Prov. 16:31), though Paul assures us in Galatians that this transformation can be speeded up as we allow ourselves to be led by the Spirit. The renovating power of God at work in us will result in real fruit: 'love, joy, peace, *patience*, kindness, goodness, faithfulness, gentleness, *self-control*' (Gal. 5:22–23, ESV, emphasis mine).

PRAYER

Lord, I pray that You will speed up the growth of Your spiritual fruit in my life. Fill me with patience and self-control today so that I can be used by You effectively in Your kingdom. Amen.

38
WITH
Nigel Watts

Safe

Luke 12:1–7; Psalm 90:1–17

Are not five sparrows sold for two pennies?
Yet not one of them is forgotten by God. **LUKE 12:6**

'We are dealing with a suspect car bomb,' the US military guard said as we pulled up, 'you'll have to find your own way into the city some other way.' It was only my third day in theatre. I had arrived at the check-point on the outskirts of Baghdad, fully expecting to be let in to the relative safety of the city itself, back to my accommodation. Having been refused entry we had to find another way back to safety. It was the dead of night. With only a pin prick of torch light, and a map of downtown Baghdad that looked as familiar as the moon, we turned around, back-tracked the wrong way up the dual carriageway and exited as soon as we could. It was utterly hopeless trying to map read. I couldn't see the map anyway. We'd wing it.

The city only had so many guarded entry points into it. Driving up a wrong road, or being observed turning around as if lost, could cost us our lives. What should have taken just minutes to get 'home' was now turning into a frantic search for safe entry points. After a couple of times turning up the wrong roads, eventually we approached a safe gate and after showing our ID we were let in.

Today's reading from Luke says that our lives are in God's hands, He knows every detail about them; even the hairs on our head are numbered. In addition to this Jesus tells us that God not only knows us intimately, but more importantly perhaps, our lives are valuable to God. He cares about us, we are precious to Him. The psalmist writes, 'Teach us to number our days, that we may gain a heart of wisdom' (Psa. 90:12), in other words, 'help us to see our lives through Your eyes'. That night was not to be the night when I was going to meet my Saviour face to face, but I have never felt so close to Him as I did then.

PRAYER

Thank You for Your care for me Lord Jesus. Help me to trust that You know and love me. Amen.

Man down

39
WITH
Olly Church

Mark 9:42–50; Psalm 124:1–8

If your hand causes you to stumble, cut it off. It is better for you to enter life maimed than with two hands to go into hell, where the fire never goes out. **MARK 9:43**

I had an unsettling time in Iraq when one of my troop sergeants was killed. As his commander in the field I had an enormous sense of responsibility and some guilt. It made me question why I was there and whether I wanted to continue with this course for my life. There were two things that helped me to get through it; firstly the inspiration of other people around me and secondly, having something else to reflect on. For me that was my Christian faith. I think that it is difficult to understand or explain those situations without faith.

Psalm 124 illustrates the nature of God's protection. Much of it hinges on the little word 'if'. *If* God had not been there then … people would have 'swallowed' us whole … the flood would have engulfed us … the torrent would have completely swept us away. On ops when death lurks nearby, there is often a heightened sense of God's protection, alongside a grief for lost comrades. Andy Smith, an Infantry Colonel, explains, 'There is something in the human spirit which draws us closer to God when we've run out of our own strength to cope with the pain and tragedy that this fallen world brings.'

As soldiers of Christ we are faced with a different set of dangers daily, many are not physical but emotional and spiritual assaults in the form of doubts and temptations. Our response when others fall into sin is often judgment, when really it should be grief; and pride in ourselves, rather than thanksgiving to God that we have escaped unscathed. We do not respond as we would if we were on a human battlefield, and yet the casualties are no less serious. In fact, as Jesus says, in the long run it would have been better for us to have lost limbs than go to hell because we fell under sin's power.

PRAYER

Lord, forgive me for the times I have not grieved for or supported others when they have been targets of a spiritual attack. Amen.

40

Anon

Character

Romans 12:1–3; Philippians 4:4–9

Do not conform to the pattern of this world, but be transformed by the renewing of your mind. Then you will be able to test and approve what God's will is – his good, pleasing and perfect will. **ROMANS 12:2**

The commander of the coalition forces in the Gulf War in 1991, General 'Stormin' Norman Schwarzkopf, once said: 'Leadership is a potent combination of strategy and character. But if you must be without one, be without the strategy.'[14] We are all defined by our character; strategies can be changed to fit the current circumstances, but humanly speaking, our character generally stays fixed. This is because we find it difficult to change the way we think. Our minds are the greenhouses for the development of our character and many of our mind-sets have been acquired in our youth. We are urged in Scripture to have the 'mind of Christ' (1 Cor. 2:16). Unlike a leopard's spots, human minds and characters can be changed by the power and grace of God who, through Jesus, desires us to be 'new creations' as we come to Him.

In today's key verse, Paul urges us to be transformed by the renewing of our mind. We do this by the choices we make about how we fill our minds, 'fill them with the good stuff' writes Paul to the Philippians (I paraphrase!). He lists a selection of character-forming, mind-transforming subjects to think about ... things that are true, honourable, just, pure, lovely, commendable, excellent and praiseworthy.

Not everything I watch, read, think and say fits these criteria ... what about you? The way we act comes from the overflow of what we think. Our character is formed inside us, in our innermost thoughts and beliefs. Our actions can build us up and strengthen us, or they can weaken or even tear down our characters because they affect the way we think.

PAUSE

What actions have you taken over the past few days that have built your character and renewed your mind? What actions do you need to take over the next few days and weeks? Write them down and put them somewhere prominent to remind you to take actions that will build up your character.

NOTES FROM THE FRONT

08 'The Wall'

BEA FISHBACK

I stood with him in front of 'the Wall'. His aged finger caressed the names engraved on it as if touching something precious. As he spoke and recounted a story, his rounded shoulders suddenly seemed a little more erect, and I was suddenly transported back in time with him ...

'... It was 6 July 1943, the place: Saipan. The men of the 105th Infantry Battalion, Company A, led by Captain Bill O'Brien and Supply Sergeant Baker, were sent to hold this small island in the South Pacific. Eighteen-year-old cousin Johnny was first running beside me and then had fallen, killed by mortar attack; flying shrapnel was striking my legs and wounding me. The enemy was too numerous and someone had to protect the men as we were pushed back to shore. The Captain and Sergeant placed themselves between the onslaught of enemy fire and the company. Sitting side by side at the last tree before the beach, they began to fire rapidly into the dense brush, screaming at us to "get the hell out of there". Running into the foam, into the waves that would eventually take us to our ship and to safety, we knew without looking behind that our leaders were dead ...'

Bea's father (bottom left)

The story ended and I was slowly aware that he and I were once again in front of the Medal of Honor wall in the Pentagon's Hall of Heroes – the wall designated to honour those men who dared to die for their country. I marvelled at the courage of those two men, Captain O'Brien and Sergeant Baker, who died at that last tree on the beach, and others like them who were willing to lay down their lives so that others could live.

It was the first time I had ever heard this story. Now it was nearly sixty years after the event in Saipan. The man at the wall, after his five years in military service and being wounded three times, would eventually return home, fall in love, and get married. He and his wife would in turn have seven children. I would be the sixth child in this family. It took a long time for my father to have the courage to speak about this episode in his life to me. But I thank God that those two men were willing to die so that not only my father could live but me and my children would live one day as well.

It brought to mind another Man and a 'tree'. This Man also took on 'enemy fire'. Not in the form of mortar attack or flying shrapnel, but by nails tearing flesh and thorns thrust into a brow, and finally by being 'crushed' to death by the entire sins of all mankind. Jesus, the God-man, hung on the cross and was willing to sacrifice His life so that others could live, not only here on earth but with His Father in paradise.

Just as the man at the wall, my father, was alive to pass this story on to other generations, so Jesus' story does not end with His death either. After three days He rose from His earthly tomb, walked with His loved ones, and then went to sit on His throne beside His heavenly Father. The story of His ultimate sacrifice for humanity was to be passed on to a thousand generations.

This is a timeless story for my family to know and understand – to never forget the sacrifice of Captain O'Brien and Sergeant Baker. But, it is only a reflection of the enormity of the sacrifice that Christ gave for each of us. He was willing to die so that each person in every family would have the choice to live for ever with Him.

41
WITH
Cole Maynard

A disciplined approach

Luke 9:1–6; Proverbs 12:1

Whoever loves discipline loves knowledge, but whoever hates correction is stupid. **PROVERBS 12:1**

Whilst on exercise in Canada I conducted a service in the field for one of the infantry companies of 1st Battalion, The Green Howards. Under the camouflage nets strung between two armoured vehicles, my dusty congregation sat on the ground whilst the Company Sergeant Major read the lesson I had given him earlier. He stood in his usual erect manner and, squinting over the pages of my Bible, ordered: 'Right, you lot, listen in!' And then in his finest Yorkshire brogue began, 'And Jesus turned to his twelve *disciplines* and told them …' All through the passage, to the amusement of some, he referred to the 'twelve *disciplines*' of Jesus, oblivious to it being '*disciples*' but reading with such authority that no one would have dared challenge this interpretation!

Yet while his reading was flawed, his insight was spot on as the word '*discipline*' is derived from '*disciple*', and to be a 'follower' of Jesus indeed requires great discipline! Discipline is defined as the 'practice of training people to follow rules or a code of behaviour'.[5] When people are trained in this way they become much stronger or more capable in that particular area or skill than they would have been without this training. Being a soldier of Christ requires no less discipline than that of a Regular, with our training being that of prayer, reading the Bible, meeting regularly with other Christians, and training our hearts and minds to focus on spiritual issues whilst not being distracted by the world around us. The undisciplined 'disciple' is a contradiction in terms and soon loses sight of the Lord he is meant to be following.

Take a few minutes today and honestly review your life. Where are you winning? Where are you losing? And what are you going to do about it?

PRAYER

Lord, help me to be a disciplined follower of You. Help me in my areas of weakness and strengthen my resolve. Show me if there are actions or training I could undertake to strengthen my ability to follow You more closely. I pray in Jesus' name. Amen.

Sentry duty

42
WITH
Rhett Parkinson

Colossians 4:2–6; Matthew 24:36–21

Devote yourselves to prayer, being watchful and thankful. **COLOSSIANS 4:2**

It had been a long slog ... two nights and days in full kit, moving tactically over the mountains of Wales. The sun was warm on our backs and there were three of us in the observation post, the remaining three in the section resting further back in the woods. I was on sentry duty, Steve was observing the enemy position and Andy was kipping in the rest position. Foolishly, I had decided that we should do an hour on each position and then rotate. My head was nodding and as I opened my sleepy eyes I saw the colour sergeant's boots ... busted! As a lesson to ourselves and the other officer cadets, we were awarded ten days ROPs (Restriction of Privileges). Lesson learnt!

Both the readings today exhort us to be watchful. In Matthew 24 Jesus urges believers to stay faithful, ready and expectant as we will not know at what hour He will return. When He returns we do not want to be caught napping from our spiritual duties. As for what these 'duties' involve, the key verse talks of devoted prayer. To devote ourselves speaks of giving one hundred percent of our interest and commitment. There are two requirements in our prayer life detailed here: prayer that is watchful and prayer that is thankful. Watchful prayer implies a sense of guarding and defending the areas of responsibility, and people, that God has entrusted to us. We can do this by speaking out scriptural promises and by asking God to send angelic reinforcements. We can ask for the protection of the Lord Jesus from all who would seek to harm us and those we love. After doing so, it is natural for our hearts to turn in thanksgiving for all that God has done. A final word of warning … I have discovered that the things I learnt on the sunny hillside in Wales hold true in my spiritual life too; the times when I am most likely to kip on duty is when I am overtired and comfortable. It is when things are all going well that I am most likely to fail to pray diligently.

PRAYER

Spend time in watchful and thankful prayer for the people and ministries God has given you.

43
WITH
Vicky Roberts

Under authority

Proverbs 3:5–6; 2 Samuel 7:18–28

Sovereign LORD, you are God! Your covenant is trustworthy, and you have promised these good things to your servant. **2 SAMUEL 7:28**

Lots of people tell me that they couldn't possibly join the Army, or any other similar organisation, because of the strict discipline. Perhaps by this they mean that they are not sure that they like the idea of other people telling them what to do! And I have to confess, there are times in my military career when my loyalty could have been questioned by others, or questioned by myself, as I tried to decide whether to follow the order or direction given (especially if I happened to disagree with it), or whether to continue along my own way. I know that this has happened most when I haven't liked or trusted the senior person or organisation giving me the direction, or when I don't feel that they have fully understood the situation, either through lack of time, willingness or inclination!

In contrast, how easy it is to obey a commander who is intelligent, trustworthy and who makes the time to understand the situation as fully as possible in the circumstances. I'm fortunate to have had a few like this. Equally, we can have absolute confidence in God as being all-knowing, completely and utterly good, holy, loving, kind, compassionate, full of integrity and with our very best interests at heart – in short, He is perfect. I wonder why then do I still sometimes struggle to trust and obey Him? David's prayer in the reading from 2 Samuel today provides a wonderful example of a heart fully submitted to the will of God. David's desire was to build God a temple. It was a good desire, but not the perfect plan God had for David. David had to go and sit before the Lord and 'talk it through'. In doing so he put into practice the heart-felt entreaty voiced in Proverbs 3:5–6, he had to 'trust in the LORD with all [his] heart, and lean not on [his] own understanding'.

PRAYER

Lord, help me in my unbelief to trust You more each day, and to obey You more readily. Amen.

What a mess!

44
WITH
Charles Kirke

Luke 1:30–37; John 10:7–10

For nothing is impossible with God. **LUKE 1:37 (NLT)**

When I arrived in the Falklands one of the first things that struck me was the rubbish; it was four years after the war and nothing dangerous was happening. But even after all that time the place was still a wreck. There were redundant barbed wire fences all over the place. There were ruined aircraft and other less obviously broken military kit. There was rubbish and debris everywhere. There were holes in the ground – craters and trenches – all around Port Stanley. Then a remarkable thing happened. A Royal Engineers regiment was deployed to 'clean the place up', a Herculean task that only the sappers really believed could be done. And it was. Three months later the rubbish was gone, the fences and debris had been removed and the place looked beautiful again.

What can we do to remove the rubbish from our own lives and to help others to do the same? Let's come before God and ask about the clutter. We've all got some! What barbed wire fences are we keeping to protect the sensitive places in our lives? Are we hanging on to broken stuff (physical or mental) that we should cast off? What gets in the way between us and Jesus? If we think it can't be got rid of, we are wrong. Nothing is impossible with God.

Jesus did not say, 'Life's a mess. Live with it,' but, 'I have come that they may have life, and have it to the full' (John 10:10). Re-read the passage from John reflecting on the picture of Jesus being the door – the way through to a new life of abundance and fullness. Look forward in prayer, asking God to show you what that richness looks like, then pause for thought and remember that it is only through Christ that this goodness is possible.

PRAYER

Lord Jesus, You see me as I am and You love me as I am, but You also see the potential that I have. Please show me where the clutter is, inspire me to ditch it, and show me how to do so in order to become more fully the person You created me to be. Amen.

45
WITH
Clive Langmead

Pier head jump

Acts 18:18–28; 1 Corinthians 3:1–23

I planted the seed, Apollos watered it, but God has been making it grow. So neither the one who plants nor the one who waters is anything, but only God, who makes things grow. **1 CORINTHIANS 3:6–7**

It was what the Royal Navy calls a 'pier head jump' – the last minute opportunity to earn some extra cash by going back to sea, in my case for some Naval Reserve training. At the time I was navigator of MV *Doulos* – an ocean liner operating on a volunteer basis for worldwide Christian mission, including book sales, shipboard conferences, and outreach programmes. As navigator I, like everyone else, was 'paid' one pound a week, as pocket money out of funds I had raised mainly through our church. Actually, I lie. Since I was on board with my wife and child we ran to two pounds!

Now back in the UK for the birth of our second child we were living in a remote shepherd's cottage and could do with two weeks' navy pay. We also needed more support. I confirmed a navy staff course which sounded ideal, but was suddenly switched to minesweeping. Joining HMS *Bickington* I was warned, 'Be careful of the XO, he's very religious.' Adrian Nance certainly proved so. We have remained friends ever since. Not least because one day as we walked down a quayside in Guernsey, he turned and said: 'I totalled my car three months ago, and I've just got the insurance. I think you should have it to navigate *Doulos*!'[6]

In Acts, we read a fascinating account of a shared partnership in which different people used their gifts consecutively for building God's kingdom. Paul began the work aided by Priscilla and Aquila. After he left, the work was taken on by Apollos. Paul refers to this time in the reading from 1 Corinthians. He emphasises that although they worked hard, the outcome didn't depend on human effort, instead God made the 'seed grow'. Sometimes I focus so much on what I can't do, that I neglect to do what God has equipped me to do. What about you?

PRAYER

Thank You Lord that once I have played my part and used my talents to care for the 'seeds', You are the one who is responsible for their growth. Amen.

NOTES FROM THE FRONT

09 The journey

ANDY SMITH

My journey began in 1999, when my wife started an Alpha course at a local church. I was happy for her but it wasn't for me; I didn't 'need' God. A year later she was baptised, it was very moving and again I was happy for her, but I still didn't need God.

After our next move, my wife went church hunting. At one, they asked her about me, and whether I had faith. My wife was gracious and very loyal. She explained that I was supportive but not committed. They even asked about our relationship. She told them it was good – well, good enough – we had two lovely young children so that was evidence of intimacy, wasn't it? Life wasn't easy with little ones; sleepless nights, coping alone with everything the Army throws at you. When I heard a church was concerned for the health of our physical relationship, I was intrigued. I agreed to accompany my wife to Spring Harvest, a Christian weekend. To be honest, I couldn't get excited about the worship in the 'Big Top'. My wife spent more time with 'church people' and seemed happier with them than with me. I became jealous and felt sidelined.

Later that year, after a six-month tour in the Balkans, I surprised my wife by returning a day early. As I came in the front door, I could hear the sounds of people chatting and laughing in our living room. My wife was hosting an Alpha course. I felt like an impostor. My wife was so happy and fulfilled but I wasn't part of it. We argued. God and the church seemed to be more important than me and the children. I kept going to church; they were decent folk but not really my sort. The teaching challenged me but I wasn't convinced.

Two years running, we holidayed at Spring Harvest in France. I enjoyed the first year, the guest speaker enjoyed marathon running and I connected with him. But the second year was a disaster; the speaker focused entirely on the power of prayer. I wasn't interested in his 24/7 prayer hut and was even more indignant when he explained that many professing Christian couples never prayed openly together at home. I felt uncomfortable and challenged; I had come to believe in Jesus but not enough for it to fill my life in that way.

Then we were posted to Germany for a nine-month stint, which brought me to my knees. My wife was depressed – my success at work was tearing her life apart with the constant moving, changing churches, schools and friends. I came home one day and saw the look in her eyes. I knew it well and it was chilling. The look of someone so beautiful on the outside and yet so empty within, an utterly wretched condition which I had no power to resolve. To compound matters, I had a job which I could do standing on my head but for no apparent reason my confidence had evaporated. Something was seriously wrong but I couldn't explain why. I kept having memories of that disastrous Spring Harvest holiday and the subject of prayer.

Lost for words and ideas to console my wife, I finally swallowed my pride, turned to her and gingerly said, 'Let's pray.' I hoped this might encourage her, but it didn't seem to elicit a positive response! I prayed anyway, a ragged prayer – not really knowing what I should say – and then a miracle happened. It wasn't a road to Damascus experience, but something tangible changed – a peace which cannot be explained came upon us and increased as the days passed. We began to pray more frequently and put our trust in God to provide for our needs. Miracles began to happen in our lives.

Sometime later, I felt the Holy Spirit was leading me to make a public declaration of my faith by getting baptised. Soon afterwards, I was notified by my regiment that I was their sole nomination for command of the regiment. However, after much prayer, I felt the Lord directing me to relinquish this opportunity. Having done so, many thought that I was preparing to leave the Army – quite the reverse. I just felt God wanted me to look after my family first and leave the rest to Him. It was actually an easy decision, although many colleagues and senior officers said it was a very courageous move.

Extraordinary blessings at work followed. Through it all, I have discovered that God has a plan for my life. Rather than trying to be in control myself of this pathway, I have found that yielding to Him has been the best decision of my life.

46
WITH
Jack Crompton
and Vicky Roberts

Wake up call!

John 9:35–41; Acts 9:1–19

Then Ananias went to the house and entered it. Placing his hands on Saul, he said, 'Brother Saul, the Lord – Jesus, who appeared to you on the road as you were coming here – has sent me so that you may see again and be filled with the Holy Spirit.' **ACTS 9:17**

When I was based in Singapore, our accommodation block was spacious to say the least. It was designed to get rid of as much heat as possible, with no glass, but large verandas and plenty of fans to assist with the airflow. In order to have some privacy we partitioned the room, using lockers as the dividing 'walls'. Our working hours were 0600 to 1300, also because of the heat. One of us was woken each morning at 0500 and we woke the next person along, before showering, dressing and eating breakfast. I woke one morning at 0505 and immediately woke my neighbour before heading to the ablutions. I had a shave and was just getting out of the shower when I heard an angry colleague asking why we were all up before 0200. Oops – I had misread the hands on the clock; instead of it being 0505 it had actually been only 0125!

In our Christian life, as in our physical life, we definitely need to have our eyes open. In today's reading from Acts we see Saul, who like the Pharisees in John 9, was spiritually blind. God grabbed his attention by making him physically blind. But that was not the end; God chose a faithful servant to open Saul's eyes spiritually, and with that came a physical healing and a transformation. Saul became Paul, the author of much of the New Testament. I wonder if there are times when you (like me!) have ignored prejudice – your own and other people's; distorted God's Word and chosen to do it in your own way? Or perhaps you've judged others by outward appearance rather than the inner person? It is so easy to put more importance on our physical appearance rather than transforming our inner selves. We need God's healing and 20/20 vision.

PRAYER

Lord God, open my eyes so I can see clearly and see myself and other people as You do. Amen.

Sleep deprivation

47
WITH
Emilie Rathbone

Exodus 20:8–11; Matthew 11:25–30

Come to me, all you who are weary and burdened, and I will give you rest. **MATTHEW 11:28**

On a particularly arduous exercise at Sandhurst, which involved digging defences in preparation for an impending attack from the enemy, our section had done well by completing the trench relatively quickly, but we had only had about four hours of sleep in two and a half days. To say I was exhausted would be an understatement! Our section was then sent out on patrol, but I was really at the limit of my tiredness. As we prepared to move off, I found myself talking to a small bush a few metres away thinking that it was one of my section! It took me a number of minutes before I realised what I was doing and by this point one of my colleagues had come over and was helping me onto my feet and pointing me in the right direction of the route. I was very embarrassed when I realised what I had done; now at least, it is something I can look back and laugh about.

The military understand the need that we all have for enough sleep and rest. They often conduct exercises which push the limits of human endurance. As a result, the troops trained through them become able to understand in a safe environment, the effect sleep deprivation has on their bodies and minds, so that in a real battle they recognise the signs and are prepared for the results. If we are going to be effective as Christian soldiers, we also need adequate sleep and rest. Getting over-tired and over-busy dulls our ability spiritually as well as our physical and emotional edge. It makes us weak targets for enemy attack. God knows this, He designed day *and* night – and bodies that needed sleep every day. He even designated a whole day of rest and made it law in the Jewish calendar – one of His top Ten Commandments – perhaps because He knew that if it was an option, human nature would simply ignore it!

PRAYER

Lord, thank You for the gift of rest. Help me to rest effectively so I can work effectively afterwards. Amen.

48

Anon

Defence of the realm

Proverbs 4:1–23; Amos 3:10–11

'My people have forgotten how to do right,' says the LORD. 'Their fortresses are filled with wealth taken by theft and violence. Therefore,' says the Sovereign LORD, 'an enemy is coming! He will surround them and shatter their defences. Then he will plunder all their fortresses.' **AMOS 3:10–11 (NLT)**

Fortresses were often built on the edge of a nation's boundaries or on the walls of a city in ancient times. They were designed to be a strong point where the enemy was turned back and the nation saved. However, they also had another less well-known role: safeguarding national treasures, their strong walls making them ideally suited to protect valuables. The Tower of London is a good example of this. It was built to protect the city and became the recipient of the Crown Jewels. Today it remains a strong citadel; the nation's royal treasures are protected by ancient sturdy walls and modern steel vaults. It is well known that the jewels are guarded heavily by modern security systems and yeomen warders. You might be mistaken in thinking that these nattily dressed individuals are just well-versed and entertaining tour guides; but they are also retired servicemen, familiar with royal duties and protocols. At night however, after the tower is closed to the public, the ceremony of the keys is performed. Then the responsibility for guarding the tower and its treasure is taken on by the Army, dressed in MTP (Multi Terrain Pattern) and armed with SA 80s. The illusion of the tower being only a museum is stripped away; now the tower is seen for the fortress it really is.

Faith in the good news of Jesus and being filled with the presence of the Holy Spirit is described in the New Testament as treasure within each one of us (see 2 Cor. 4:7). Not the ill-gotten gains of theft and violence Amos talks of, but the precious deposit of God that will remain sure to the very end (1 Pet. 1:7). It is our responsibility to guard it to keep the fortress secure, protecting the treasure within. Proverbs 4:23 states the case strongly, 'Above all else,' it says, 'guard your heart, for everything you do flows from it.'

PRAYER

Lord, show me how to guard my heart and its valuable treasure. Thank You for the extra protection that Your Holy Spirit provides. Amen.

Camaraderie

49
WITH
Vicky Roberts

1 John 2:15–17; James 4:1–4

don't you know that friendship with the world means enmity against God? Therefore, anyone who chooses to be a friend of the world becomes an enemy of God. **JAMES 4:4**

During basic training at Sandhurst, it was not uncommon to be ironing or washing the floor at one o'clock in the morning. However ridiculous this may sound now, it didn't seem too unreasonable then, as my fellow officer cadets were engaged in similar activities at the same time. Somehow this seemed to make things better and perhaps even seem normal!

In the Christian journey we might also find ourselves doing things that are considered to be weird by the world, things such as prayer, Bible reading, or acts of kindness or humility – often counter-cultural in the often alpha-male environment of the Armed Forces. This might lead us to disguise our Christian habits, or worse still to stop doing them completely. If surrounded by behaviour which is not honouring to the Lord, we can find ourselves slipping further away from God's will, believing it to be quite acceptable as apparently 'everyone's doing it'. Like the frog who was unaware of the water being slowly heated, we too can become desensitised to harmful practices, meaning that we fail to jump out before it is too late.

The solution is simple: we must ensure that we are linked into a network of people with whom we can be truthful and accountable. Preferably these should be people who are close enough to meet with face to face and who may be able to rein us in when they see or hear things in us which we may not recognise ourselves. If this is not possible, we must find friends who will pray faithfully for us and whom we can phone, text or email to keep them updated. The AFCU has associate prayer groups for this very reason. Finally, the Holy Spirit acts as our Encourager, to help us to choose the narrow path and to walk faithfully on it.

PRAYER

Lord, thank You that You do not leave us alone but send Your Holy Spirit to be with us. Help us to not go it alone but to choose godly companions and to have the courage and integrity to follow Your will. Amen.

50

Anon

VC

Matthew 5:14–16; 1 Timothy 4:1–13

Don't let anyone look down on you because you are young, but set an example for the believers in speech, in conduct, in love, in faith and in purity. **1 TIMOTHY 4:12**

The epitaph for Jack Cornwell, aged sixteen, one of the youngest Victoria Cross (VC) winners, reads: 'It is not wealth or ancestry but honourable conduct and a noble disposition that maketh men great.' Jack served as a Boy 1st Class on HMS *Chester* during the Battle of Jutland (31 May 1916). He remained at his post as a sight-setter despite receiving mortal wounds early in the battle, patiently awaiting further orders until the end of the action. Other reports tell how despite his wounds, he volunteered to go to the turret to wipe the glass for the range finder. Jack died two days later in hospital in Humber. He was recommended for a posthumous VC because of the example he set others of steadfast attention to duty.

In today's key verse Paul says to Timothy: 'Don't let anyone look down on you because you are young, but set an example for the believers'. Age, rank and inexperience do not disqualify us from being an example to others in the way we live for Christ. Believers are encouraged by Jesus to remember that they are 'light-bearers', and need to live in such a way that the world 'may see your good deeds and glorify your Father in heaven' (Matt. 5:16). For Jack Cornwell this meant remaining at his post and doing his duty for as long as it was physically possible. Selflessly he put the needs of others before his own and in doing so set the pattern for other servicemen and women to follow. This inspiring story challenges me to ask myself as a soldier of Christ, 'Where am I bringing glory to God by the way I live and the example I set?' What about you?

PRAYER

Father God, forgive me for the times I have used age, position and inexperience as an excuse to hold back from living my life the way You want me to. Help me to remember that I am tasked to bear Your light to a dark world. May I stand at my post no matter what happens. Amen.

NOTES FROM THE FRONT

10 Mediterranean rescue

MARK LEAKEY

In the late 1990s I commanded an RAF Harrier squadron which was deployed – in response to Saddam Hussein's sabre rattling – aboard the Royal Navy's aircraft carrier HMS *Invincible*, in the Mediterranean. I led the first night training mission. It was one of those sorties I should never have flown. Everything went wrong. It was a night, low altitude bombing detail on the ship's splash target, using night vision goggles and the aircraft's forward looking infrared system. Reasonably challenging at the best of times. But the weather was awful, the infrared system wasn't doing much for me and I had been working for some 20 days without a break.

The ship was completely blacked out; the adrenaline was flowing. At the end of the sortie I got high on the approach to the hover and over-corrected. I could not stop the rate of descent and crashed into the sea alongside the ship. I briefly lost consciousness on impact. Somehow I survived the crash but came to with a certain knowledge that I was drowning. I thought I was still in the cockpit.

Somehow, instinctively, I did the only things that could have saved me – I undid the ejection seat straps, released the parachute harness and pulled the life jacket toggle. I surfaced gasping for breath. After about an hour I was rescued by a Royal Navy helicopter.

What I did not realise was that the aircraft had rolled on its back and the ejection seat had fired me down into the water. I have no recollection to this day of pulling the seat firing handle. I should not have survived the impact; but having survived that, I should never have survived being ejected down into the sea.

I had a routine scan of my injured back; for some reason the radiologist scanned my head as well. A short while later I experienced one of those sorts of moments we all dread: the doctor sat me down and told me that I had cancer – a brain tumour.

I was instantly grounded, I lost my medical flying category and two weeks after that I lost command of my squadron. I had been rescued – but for what? The first prognosis was not comforting – I could be dead within nine months. The maximum the neurosurgeon gave me was five to ten years. There was nothing he could do for me.

I went to ground for six months. Why had God allowed all this to happen to me? What would happen to my wife and two sons after I died? And more immediately would I be court-martialled? But actually it was an extraordinary time – a time of great peace, knowing that God had my future in His hands. And here I am, some sixteen years later, still alive; bizarrely the RAF promoted me and gave me some tip-top jobs before I took early retirement and started working for the AFCU. And I'm still deeply conscious of God's hands of rescue in my life, not only a physical rescue but also, and far more significantly, a spiritual rescue from sin and despair.

Mark in the cockpit

51

WITH

Tim Symonds

Posting preference

Philippians 2:12–18; Jeremiah 29:1–14

Do everything without grumbling or arguing, so that you may become blameless and pure, 'children of God without fault in a warped and crooked generation.' Then you will shine among them like stars in the sky **PHILIPPIANS 2:14–15**

I was serving in England in the late sixties. I had applied for the language course at the MOD Chinese Language School in Hong Kong, but the posting order I received was for Germany. Not only did I not want to go, but I felt I was not suited to the job at all, and so I did all I could to protest. It was to no avail, although my 'wish' to do the language course was 'noted'. It was with reluctance therefore that I grasped the prickly nettle and reported for duty. However, as I did so I had an amazing sense of assurance that all would work out, especially as far as going to Hong Kong was concerned. The job was as tough as I had feared, but God sent a marvellous young officer to work alongside me who was a tremendous help and, in time, God used me in turn to show him the way to Christ. He joined the OCU (now AFCU) and some years later entered the Anglican ministry. I had many other wonderful opportunities that I would not have done, had my wish been granted to go to Hong Kong. Looking back I regretted the objections I had made to the posting, especially my lack of trust that God was in overall control; I felt I let Him down by my protests.

Paul encourages the Philippians to do everything without complaining! A hard task when we feel that things are not going the way they should for us. It is particularly hard when we feel that a specific direction for our lives has been blocked. I have found it is at times like this when God's promise made to the exiles in Babylon is of special comfort; God says, 'I know the plans I have for you ... plans to prosper you and not to harm you, plans to give you hope and a future' (Jer. 29:11).

PRAYER

Lord, help me to trust You when life makes no sense to me. Amen.

O Group

52
WITH
Rhett Parkinson

John 10:11–32; Hebrews 3:7–14

My sheep listen to my voice; I know them, and they follow me. **JOHN 10:27**

Whilst commanding an armoured engineer squadron I deployed on exercise in Canada supporting an armoured infantry battle-group (BG). I had the privilege of being an integral part of the BG planning team, advising the CO as his engineer SME, as well as leading over 160 men and women mounted in tracked and wheeled vehicles. Having received brigade orders, we would follow the estimate process extracting the relevant orders and coming up with a plan for the BG. While the rest of the planning team then got their 'heads down', I would drive to wherever the squadron was leaguered, write and then give my officers their orders in a squadron O Group. They would then extract the relevant bits and pass orders to their vehicle commanders whilst I headed back to find the CO, often arriving just in time to launch the next operation.

All members of the military understand the need for a clearly given orders process; it enables the various actions to reflect the commander's intent. Jesus says in today's reading that we can hear His voice just like sheep know the voice of their shepherd. God wants us to hear Him speak clearly, so that our actions here on earth are fulfilling His intent; *His* kingdom come, *His* will be done on earth as it is in heaven.

God speaks to us in many ways. These include hearing Him through His written Word; through other people; through His creation and through the prompting of that 'inner voice'. There are two problems with hearing God's voice. The first is caused not by God being silent, but by us not listening. Listening can take time, concentration and deliberate stopping to hear before moving out. Sometimes when others speak I confess I am not actually listening to what they have to say; instead I am rehearsing my reply. The other problem we face is not that we don't hear God speak, but that we don't like what He has to say!

PAUSE

Has God given you any 'orders' which you have chosen to ignore? Deal with it today in repentance and fresh obedience as befitting a soldier of Christ.

53

Anon

No sign of the enemy

Psalm 31:24; Job 5:19–27

From six calamities he will rescue you; in seven no harm will touch you. In famine he will deliver you from death, and in battle from the stroke of the sword. **JOB 5:19–20**

During a tour in Iraq in 2007 my squadron had to drive through a city known to be a hot-bed of insurgents. The local coalition commander in that area told me that they no longer entered the city because of the high number of casualties they had sustained. The enemy were well armed and could be expected to attack us with mines, sniper fire, rockets and anti-tank weapons. For our protection we had limited armoured vehicles, soft-skinned Land Rovers and two helicopter gunships on either side. The night before we were due to leave, I remember thinking that I should write to my wife and children telling them of my love for them, in case I should not return. However, as I began to write I felt a check in my spirit – my God is mighty to save. I rose up and declared He is the same yesterday, today and forever. He will protect us, save us and deliver us.

As we approached the town, six police cars erupted from the city gate tearing past us as if fleeing for their lives. We continued and drove four kilometres through the town. It was eerie. Not a soul on the streets. Not a dog barked. Not a shot fired. We came through unscathed. A staff officer at Divisional HQ told me later that fearing for our lives, he could not get out of bed the next morning because he dreaded hearing the news of the massacre that must have taken place. The commander of the insurgents was, we heard, summarily sacked. The Lord had put fear into the hearts of the enemy just as He did to win battles in Old Testament times.

King David was no stranger to God's protection in combat. His troops won many battles; these are recorded in 2 Samuel 8:6 as being won with the help of the Lord: 'The LORD gave David victory wherever he went.' His eloquent prayer is recorded in our reading today from Psalm 31, in which he reiterates his confidence and trust in God at a time when he was feeling old, weak and vulnerable (see vv9–10). Most importantly of all he clings to an important truth, 'My times are in your hands' (v15). Soldiers of Christ need to know that their lives are governed by the will of God.

PAUSE

Be strong and take heart, all you who hope in the LORD (Psa. 31:24).

Final orders

54
WITH
Charles Kirke

Matthew 28:16–20; Romans 10:8–15

All authority in heaven and on earth has been given to me. Therefore go and make disciples of all nations, baptising them in the name of the Father and of the Son and of the Holy Spirit, and teaching them to obey everything I have commanded you. **MATTHEW 28:18–20**

Robert was being an absolute pain. He was determined to get my wife and I to a Christian fellowship meeting at his house and, frankly, we didn't want to go. It was not our scene. We believed and went to church, but we didn't do that stuff – Bible bashing and all that. But he wouldn't stop asking. Over and over again! It became a sort of joke between us. He must have had the thickest skin ever, and stacks of determination. And then he had a brainwave. He invited us to supper on the day of the next meeting and sheer politeness meant that we just couldn't refuse. Nor when it was over could we just get up from the table and escape the meeting without being really rude, so we didn't. I am so grateful to Robert for his persistence and his refusal to be discouraged. That very evening we discovered the importance of Christian fellowship and the joy of being together with fellow Christians. More than thirty years later we are still discovering new things in fellowship.

Jesus' orders to us are in Matthew 28:18–20, today's key verse. Sometimes the making of disciples of all nations starts right where we are, as Robert saw. Often it starts with fellowship, so let's go after fellowship when we can and encourage those who are reluctant and the unaware. After all, as Paul points out, 'how can they believe in the one of whom they have not heard? And how can they hear without someone preaching to them?' (Rom. 10:14). Of course, reaching out in this way will require sensitivity and tact, and for me this is often not the issue. Rather, I lack the determination to press in, in the face of often quite mild rejection and defensiveness. What about you?

PRAYER

Lord, give us sensitivity and determination in calling people to share fellowship, but give us a thick skin when we need it. Amen.

For more information on the Armed Forces' Christian Union, see page 170.

55

Anon

Solid as a rock

Deuteronomy 32:1–4; 2 Samuel 22:31–37

I will proclaim the name of the LORD. Oh, praise the greatness of our God! He is the Rock, his works are perfect, and all his ways are just. A faithful God who does no wrong, upright and just is he. **DEUTERONOMY 32:3–4**

Battle Back is a military organisation that helps wounded, injured or sick (WIS) service personnel to recover and rehabilitate in order to regain some skills and confidence through team-building and challenge. A friend of mine was instructing on a rock-climbing expedition with them. Unfortunately, during one of the climbs, the rock face gave way. He fell quite a distance, hitting his head badly, breaking his scapula and tibia and being knocked unconscious. The WIS soldiers reacted quickly to assist him as best as they could, calling the mountain rescue and administering emergency first aid. One of them even found this easier to do so sitting down and without his artificial leg, which he quickly discarded and laid to one side. When the Spanish mountain rescue arrived they were rather perturbed to see someone with a missing limb, imagining the incident to be far more serious than first reported. It was only after a while they realised the leg had been lost previously and it was the chap with all his limbs who needed the help!

In life, as well as when rock climbing, we need to be sure that the rock is solid and will take the strain of our weight. We need to choose our path carefully, select people in whom we trust, discard things which hinder our progress and to be anchored to things which are secure. God is frequently described as the Rock, especially in times of trouble, and a safe place for us at all times. He is the same yesterday, today and forever. He never changes and is completely faithful to us, always.

PAUSE

Today, bring yourself into the presence of the Holy and Almighty God. Ask Him to highlight to you areas of your life which are not completely abandoned to His way and for you to trust Him in everything. And to fill you with a courage and trust in Him which will enable you to continue your daily journey, and to achieve whatever goals He has in store for you.

NOTES FROM THE FRONT

11 Whether I live or die …

ANDREW MCMAHON

I am very aware of how the Lord has His hand over the way I do my job. I always pray for safety but actually I am not unduly concerned about that, as I know that whether I live or die I belong to the Lord. Having served on operations with a number of very devout Christians who have either died or been badly injured I know that even though God promises to protect us, sometimes it is not in His will. However, He always promises us His presence and peace, and the testimonies I have heard from the individuals or families affected by injury or the death of a Christian serviceman or woman is witness to God's love and care.

During Herrick IV, when the conflict was really escalating, I was based in FOB Robinson. During that time, I learnt what it meant to fire my weapon in anger. I vividly recall one occasion when a group of about twenty or thirty Taliban attacked the FOB and a fairly epic battle followed, lasting an hour and a half. To me, as a young man it seemed fairly exciting, adrenaline-pumping stuff; the sort of thing I had joined up for.

The next day, however, we were involved in another contact and I felt totally different. The attack seemed better coordinated and more audacious. My enthusiasm and courage was lacking to say the least! I grabbed my gear and sprinted to the Snatch Land Rover link-up with the Afghan National Army to coordinate their response. Before I got into the vehicle I paused. Filled with a sense of foreboding and dread I remember thinking that this could be it. My next talk with God could be face to face! I squeezed my eyes as tight as I could and prayed, 'Lord, it feels different today. I pray that this will pass over and I pray that we will survive, but if we don't, then I could be in front of You in the next forty-five minutes. I want to say that I am sorry for all the wrong things I have done. I know that You will forgive my sins because of what Jesus has done. So protect me if You will, but if not, Your will be done. And help my family to cope with my loss.' Eyes open, I buckled my chin strap and gave the nod to my sombre corporal, who drove us to the forward positions.

I can't remember the rest of the events of the day very clearly as we pressed the enemy back. What I do remember is the sense I had of God's peace, regardless of the outcome. If you are reading this today and don't know the kind of peace I am talking about, the sort you can have right now about your eternal future, then I urge you to stop and do something about it. God knows everything about you, and He loves you so much that He sent His Son Jesus to live and die for you. On the cross Jesus carried every wrong deed, action and belief that has ever been committed – including all of yours and all of mine. The Bible calls this sin. Jesus repeatedly said that we all have to repent. If we repent, that is turn away, from all that we have done wrong, and rely on Jesus, God's Son, God will forgive us. Not only will we be forgiven, which is more than we deserve, but God has said we will become His children and live with Him for ever. Finally, we need to ask God to fill us with His Holy Spirit so that we can start living our eternal life from today.

All of this can all be achieved by praying a simple prayer like the one opposite, and then choosing from now on to live a new kind of life as a follower of Jesus.

PRAYER

Father God, my life is a mess. I have wronged You in thought, word and deed.

Spend a minute saying sorry for anything that comes to mind.

I know that You sent Your Son Jesus to die on the cross for me and that You have forgiven all my sin.
Change me, so that I may lose the desire to sin.
I accept Your will for my life.
From now on I will follow You.
Please fill me with Your Holy Spirit, so that I can live the fullness of life You have for me.
In Jesus' name I pray.
Amen.

If you have prayed this prayer for the first time, find another Christian to talk to about it.

To grow in your faith you will need to read the Bible, pray regularly and find a church where you can receive support and fellowship from other believers.[7]

Moral dilemma

56

Anon

Genesis 22:1–18; 1 Corinthians 1:18–31

Where is the one who is wise? Where is the scribe? Where is the debater of this age? Has not God made foolish the wisdom of the world? **1 CORINTHIANS 1:20 (NRSV)**

When I was undergoing my selection process for the Royal Navy at the Admiralty Interview Board, I was asked if I could kill someone. 'I don't know,' I replied, 'I have never tried it, but imagine that I could in the right circumstances.' I had had to resolve this important moral question beforehand, especially from a Christian faith perspective. Even though, in a naval warfare context, only very few personnel are directly involved in the firing of a missile or torpedo from the ship's ops room; I felt that by joining the naval 'military machine' that I was indirectly involved, despite the fact I was not part of the warfare branch. Consequently, not only did I distinguish between the legitimate taking of the life of another – for example in self-defence – from an unlawful act of murder (which is how I understand this part of the Ten Commandments), but I also had to decide whether or not I had confidence in those who would be in command over me.

What moral dilemmas do you face in your life? In the reading today, Abraham was asked to kill his son Isaac and, having struggled with the moral dilemma, he set off in obedience. How he must have questioned the logic of God in this scenario. After all, God had originally promised that Abraham would have a son. Then, some years later, God seemed to ask Abraham to kill his son! The Bible tells us that God's thoughts and ways are not the same as ours (see Isa. 55:8–9). However, as we saw on Day 55, in the reading from 2 Samuel 22:31, they are 'perfect', meaning they are for our good. Often we find Him using counter-cultural methods like Jesus' death on the cross, elaborated on in the reading from 1 Corinthians. Trust in God, have full confidence in Him and in His Word; sacrifice your will to His and He will work miracles through you – sometimes in mysterious ways!

PRAYER

Lord, You know the moral dilemmas I face. Help me to trust You and to see Your hand at work. Amen.

57

WITH

Vicky Roberts

'Small' arms?

1 Samuel 17:1–58; Hebrews 12:1–2

Then Saul dressed David in his own tunic. He put a coat of armour on him and a bronze helmet on his head. David fastened on his sword over the tunic and tried walking around, because he was not used to them. 'I cannot go in these,' he said to Saul, 'because I am not used to them.' So he took them off. **1 SAMUEL 17:38–39**

On one of the exercises in training I was nominated to carry the anti-tank weapon. You might think that this put me at an advantage to close with and defeat the enemy, and so it should have done. But the truth is that, when added to the weight of my own personal equipment, I was carrying more than half of my body weight. The result was that once I got down 'on the ground' I couldn't get up under my own strength but instead lay there like a squashed beetle and was reliant on my fellow platoon members to lift me to my feet, to enable me to continue patrolling! What had been intended as a weapon to defeat the enemy had actually defeated me before the enemy was anywhere near.

In today's reading, David also felt as though he would have been weighed down with armour intended to help him, and instead chose to fight Goliath with the tools he had been given by God, his fitness and agility, his accuracy with a slingshot and his faith in God as Victor and Saviour of the Israelites. Sometimes I try to emulate leaders I admire, forgetting that God has gifted me uniquely for the role he has chosen me to fulfil. In Hebrews 12:1–2 we are also encouraged to 'throw off everything that hinders and the sin that so easily entangles' and to run our individual races with our eyes fixed on Jesus.

PAUSE

Consider today the things which might be entangling you and preventing you from running the race that God has intended for you. Ask God to help you to trust Him more fully, to help you to identify anything which is hindering you and to have the courage to discard it and to progress more fully with Him in all areas of your life.

Risky business

58
WITH
Jonny Palmer

Ecclesiastes 11:1–6; 1 Samuel 17:20–50

Cast your bread upon the waters, for you will find it after many days. **ECCLESIASTES 11:1 (NKJV)**

As a pilot in the RAF, I am not a risk averse type. When the pressure is on, danger is pressing in and the adrenaline is building, I often feel like I am having the time of my life! I think that would be true of most members of the Armed Forces. I remember one time when I was approaching our final destination in Afghanistan and the airspace was really busy. Not only that, but the ground was teaming with potential threats: cars, motorbikes, and villages. In cases like these, we liked to get the aircraft down as quickly as possible. On this occasion air traffic control started giving us a stream of orders requiring us to make changes to our altitude and track. For fifteen minutes in the cockpit every nerve was stretched and the adrenaline was pumping as we wondered if we would be able to land safely, or whether someone might take a pot-shot at the sitting grey duck overhead. It was great!

However, strangely, I don't like taking certain risks in the Christian faith, probably because I may be seen to be, or thought of as foolish. When I think that that is a very real possibility, I become very risk averse! Rather than taking the risk and 'casting my bread upon the waters', I become like the cautious man talked about in Ecclesiastes 11:4, who continually put off sowing and reaping his crops just in case the weather changed! This is not my normal default setting; it stifles my faith and restricts my growth. I wonder how David felt as he squared up to Goliath's taunts. Did he feel the fear and do it anyway? Or perhaps, he had built his faith 'muscle power' in the quiet unobserved time alone with the Lord and the sheep, so that when the time came he was ready to take the risk in the power of the Lord Almighty. This is the type of faith I want to have, how about you?[8]

PRAYER

Lord, help me to 'cast my bread upon the waters' in a no-holds-barred way to bring glory to Your kingdom. Amen.

59

WITH

Rhett Parkinson

Combat fitness

Luke 24:36–49; Acts 1:1–2:4

I am going to send you what my Father has promised; but stay in the city until you have been clothed with power from on high. **LUKE 24:49**

The use and design of body armour has come a long way since the First and Second World Wars, where it was restricted to the standard issue of a metal helmet. Today, modern soldiers are issued a comprehensive kit, comprising heavy Kevlar plates and even 'blast proof pants' – a layer of knitted silk providing protection to the pelvic region. This armour is often heavy to wear and carry, but has saved multiple lives in theatres such as Afghanistan and Iraq. In order to move and fight effectively in this kit, modern soldiers need to be extremely fit, and accustomed to both the climate and the weight of the equipment. During the training phase for a tour to Afghanistan, my regiment undertook extra training in the form of long marches, carrying more weight than required in order to build up strength. In doing so we repeated the lessons of history; in Ancient Rome, gladiators would often train with weapons heavier than those they would actually use in combat.

David discovered when he put on Saul's armour that he could not use it, as he had not developed the muscle strength and stamina needed. Instead, he chose to trust in a greater power, that of the strength of the Lord. Often I am impatient and try to do things in my own strength. Worse still, I am often not keen to put in the time, effort and discipline it would take to build up my spiritual muscle power so that, when the time comes, I am strong enough. After His resurrection, Jesus gave a specific command to His disciples, 'stay in the city until you have been clothed with power from on high'. We see that the waiting period was not passive; they actively built spiritual strength by prayer and fellowship. What can I learn from this? It is simple … wait constructively for God's timing and until He decides that I am ready. Then go, dressed not in my own ability, but in His power.

PRAYER

Lord, please help me prepare and wait for Your timing. Amen.

No ammo!

60
WITH
Charles Kirke

Matthew 25:1–46; 1 Peter 5:6–11

Be alert and of sober mind. Your enemy the devil prowls around like a roaring lion looking for someone to devour. **1 PETER 5:8**

North Belfast, 1976. It was a routine patrol – very routine. We turned left at the gate and went up the Crumlin Road to regimental HQ as we did every other day and nothing ever happened. If we had turned right, we would have gone directly into the heart of the Ardoyne and the adrenaline would have flowed like there's no tomorrow (and there was always the feeling that for us there really might be no tomorrow). But this time we turned left. Yawn!

I was wedged in the roof hatch with my head out of the vehicle, watching for the dodgy stuff that we knew wasn't going to happen on that journey. The shock came when I glanced down at my rifle. No magazine. Somehow I had done all my weapon drills and still managed to go on patrol with an empty weapon. And I was supposed to be providing top cover for my mates.

How often do we set out with our spiritual weapons unloaded? Even if things feel slack spiritually we need still to be on our guard, asking, and answering, important questions such as 'What spiritual arc should I be covering?', 'Am I fully loaded with God's Word?', 'What does God want me to do now?', 'What's my target?', 'What needs to be covered in prayer?', 'Who are my mates in this situation?', 'How am I supposed to be covering them?', 'Who is covering me?', 'When did I last see them, and when did we last share God's Word together and pray for each other?' and 'What's my blind side?' Why do we need answers to these questions? Because, as the key verse reminds us, we have a deadly enemy who is planning our destruction. Just like the bridesmaids in today's reading from Matthew 25, we must ensure that we don't get caught unawares, but that we are ready and fully-equipped for every eventuality.

PRAYER

Lord, let me be ready and fully loaded at all times.
Please grip me when I'm not. Amen.

NOTES FROM THE FRONT

12 The Soldier's Psalm

Psalm 91, often known affectionately as the 'Soldier's Psalm' is a testimony of the unknown author's faith and trust in God's infinite care and protection on the battlefield and in the barracks.

It is often used to form the basis of a prayer of faith and a litany of praise. Sometimes it has even been printed on DPM fabric ready for sewing inside the combat-jackets of troops deploying on operations.

Whoever dwells in the shelter of the Most High
  will rest in the shadow of the Almighty.
I will say of the LORD, 'He is my refuge and my fortress,
  my God, in whom I trust.'

Surely he will save you
  from the fowler's snare
  and from the deadly pestilence.
He will cover you with his feathers,
  and under his wings you will find refuge;
  his faithfulness will be your shield and rampart.
You will not fear the terror of night,
  nor the arrow that flies by day,
nor the pestilence that stalks in the darkness,
  nor the plague that destroys at midday.
A thousand may fall at your side,
  ten thousand at your right hand,
  but it will not come near you.
You will only observe with your eyes
  and see the punishment of the wicked.

If you say, 'The LORD is my refuge,'
  and you make the Most High your dwelling,
no harm will overtake you,
  no disaster will come near your tent.
For he will command his angels concerning you
  to guard you in all your ways;
they will lift you up in their hands,
  so that you will not strike your foot against a stone.
You will tread on the lion and the cobra;
  you will trample the great lion and the serpent.

'Because he loves me,' says the LORD, 'I will rescue him;
  I will protect him, for he acknowledges my name.
He will call on me, and I will answer him;
  I will be with him in trouble,
  I will deliver him and honour him.
With long life I will satisfy him
  and show him my salvation.'

PSALM 91

61

Anon

Eclat

2 Corinthians 8:1–12; Matthew 22:34–40

But since you excel in everything – in faith, in speech, in knowledge, in complete earnestness and in the love we have kindled in you – see that you also excel in this grace of giving. **2 CORINTHIANS 8:7**

'The Reds approach the crowd in tight formation, wings just feet apart, manoeuvring at speeds of up to 400 mph (720 kph). With split-second timing, releasing their trademark coloured trails, they fan out to form a perfect pattern in the sky – the Vixen Break. Rising vertically, the pilots pull a gruelling 7G, clenching their stomach muscles to help withstand the force. From the ground, it looks absolutely amazing. No wonder the Red Arrows have come to represent so much of what the RAF is about: total teamwork based on mutual trust, incredible skill put to the test, a dedication to training and excellence – plus the thrill of adventure.'[9] As a fast-jet pilot myself, I have come to value the Red Arrows motto of *eclat*, meaning 'excellence' as a standard to live by.

Excellence is a common theme in the pages of the Bible. Without pursuing it, our faith can become half-hearted and lukewarm. Paul urges the Corinthians to excel in all things including, rather surprisingly, in their giving. This is not the appeal of the TV evangelist wanting to make a quick buck, but a plea for the Corinthian disciples to love the Lord with all their heart, soul, mind ... and wallet! It seemed the Corinthians, like so many of us, needed some prompting to excel in *every area* of their lives. To be a fast-jet pilot requires hours of training, absolute dedication motivated by a love and passion for the job. Jesus asks that His soldiers are no less whole-hearted: 'Love the Lord your God with all your heart and with all your soul and with all your mind' (Matt. 22:37). This is the first and greatest commandment. 'And the second is like it: Love your neighbour as yourself.'

PRAYER

Lord, I choose *eclat* – excellence in You; putting You first in all things, and loving others the way You love me. Help me even to do this in the area of my wallet! Amen.

Prior preparation and planning?

62
WITH
Kevin Shaw

John 16:1–15; Mark 13:1–23

But when he, the Spirit of truth, comes, he will guide you into all the truth. He will not speak on his own; he will speak only what he hears, and he will tell you what is yet to come. **JOHN 16:13**

On the occasion that I was organising a week of sailing with different Christians speaking each evening, I found particular difficulty in arranging a speaker for the Thursday night. People just weren't available. As the week drew closer, I eventually found someone and thanked God … until three days before when they had to cancel. I was extremely busy running everything and had no time to spend ringing round. I had exhausted all my options; I knew I just had to pray and trust God to find someone. As the Wednesday evening arrived, I faced the realisation that I could no longer pretend that something was sorted. It had to be me! I prayed earnestly that evening, but I still had no clear ideas. On the Thursday afternoon, (God relented and) in a chance conversation, I recognised a need I could address. With no time to prepare notes, I could only trust, like Paul, that God would place the right words in my mouth. And how He did! I was enabled to speak earnestly from the heart, with a sincerity that deeply impacted several others too. God taught me much that day; not least that He can use us powerfully to answer our own prayers.

Both of today's readings contain some of the last things that Jesus said to His disciples before His death. In them He warns them about future events, giving them signs so that they will recognise the times in which they live. It is nail-biting stuff! However, in the midst of it all, the threats, the persecution and the natural signs, there is comfort. Wherever they (and we!) are, and whenever these things happen, Jesus promised then and the promise still holds, 'it is from me that he will receive what he will make known to you' (John 16:14).

PAUSE

What divine help do you need today? Ask Jesus to send His Holy Spirit to give you the right words to speak.

63
WITH
Nigel Watts

Supply line

Psalm 50:1–23; Luke 12:27–40

for every animal of the forest is mine,
and the cattle on a thousand hills. **PSALM 50:10**

'What is stopping you Nigel?' Simon asked me pointedly. 'If God is calling you to leave the Army, He will provide.' The conversation had taken place at New Wine[10] in 2006. However, God had been on my case for the past ten years. During the week, God put His finger on my reluctance to leave the Army: money. It was all about trusting God with my money. I was the typical Army guy. I had a mortgage to pay, three kids at boarding school aged fifteen, thirteen and eleven. Precept, the Christian Charity I felt called to work for, could not even afford to pay me a salary. Humanly speaking, it was madness to even contemplate it. However, God didn't give up. He spoke to me again about trusting Him financially. That was it. Within days I had resigned.

When He calls, He provides. This is my testimony. My third son left school in the summer of 2013. God provided for each of our boys, who amazingly stayed on at their schools. One of the names of God in the Bible is Yahweh Yireh, meaning He is the Lord who provides. It is in God's very nature to provide for us when we are faithful to His will. After all, He has the resources to do it; as the psalmist says, He owns all the cattle on the hills. Jesus elaborates on the trustworthy nature of God in the reading from Luke. In it He tells us to 'seek his kingdom' (Luke 12:31) rather than earthly security. When we do so, all of our other needs will be provided for; in other words God gives us the minimum of what we need and then some more. This is not a 'prosperity gospel', this is the generous nature of a loving father. In my case, I am as amazed as anyone else *how* He has done it. But, this I know, He is an incredible God and worthy of all our praise.

PRAYER

Father, please help me learn what it means to seek first Your kingdom and Your righteousness, and to let go of my fear of being without. Amen.

Re-gain

64
WITH
Vicky Roberts

Exodus 17:8–16; Galatians 6:1–3

Aaron and Hur held his hands up – one on one side, one on the other – so that his hands remained steady till sunset. **EXODUS 17:12B**

Whilst I quite enjoy most aspects of physical training and assault courses, the one element that I dread is the rope 're-gain'. I can manoeuvre myself along a rope quite well when I've got both my hands and feet securely around it, but once I lose my grip with either my hands or my feet, I struggle to be able to get my own body weight back onto the rope and usually end up 'in the abyss'.

Life can be like that too. Whilst everyday issues may leave us feeling slightly battered and bruised, we can usually carry on OK. Sometimes though, our habits, or standards, slip or fall too far either through neglect or complete exhaustion, and we cannot do the re-gain ourselves. At these times, rather than fall into the abyss, we need to rely on God and our fellow Christians, to share our burdens, lift us back on track and enable us to carry on our journey. In Exodus 17, Moses was unable to keep his hands raised when he grew tired, and relied on Aaron and Hur to raise his hands, allowing the Israelites to prevail in the fight against the Amalekites. In the same way we need to support one another through prayer, example, and practical help. Galatians 6 warns us to watch out for others, and for ourselves, so that we are not caught out by sin, and carry each other's burdens.

As you read the reflection today you may be struggling at the moment and feel that you are about to lose your grip in certain areas. Ask God for help to identify the people whom He has put around you who are ready to assist, and for Him to gently restore you. Equally, today you may be in a position of strength. If so, watch out for those around you who may need help to get back on the straight and narrow, and offer that helping hand.

PRAYER

Lord, show me the people around me who
I should pay attention to. Amen.

65

Anon

Barracks

Colossians 3:12–17; Deuteronomy 20:1–3

Whatever you do, work at it with all your heart, as working for the Lord, not for human masters **COLOSSIANS 3:23**

For the media, the exploits of the Armed Forces are most newsworthy when they are deployed on operations. The reality is though, that all military personnel spend the vast majority of their time at home in barracks. For much of the time, despite wearing uniform, most of the jobs performed are routine, ordinary, even dull. Jobs that most average civilians can and do perform every day.

In a similar way the spiritual soldier spends much time on mundane and ordinary living. While trying to do everything for the glory of God, family life, work and other activities fill each day in normal routines. This can make the believer feel that their faith is ineffective when sometimes it is just routine. Of course, this does not deny the need to guard against complacency. However, as the military knows well, the standards and examples that are set in barracks, condition the type of behaviour that happens when deployed. In addition to this the outlook of the ship's captain or the CO will fundamentally affect the choices made by those they command. When the pressure is on, these normal patterns of behaviour, developed in slow time, will be tested to the utmost.

The same is true during times of spiritual adversity. It is only when we have put in the ordinary routine daily tasks, including our regular prayer and reading of God's Word, that we will be able to face battle without fear, knowing that God is fighting with us and for us as the reading from Deuteronomy shows. Paul reminds us in the New Testament that we are not seeking to please an earthly employer but our spiritual Captain. He is the one whose example could, and will, affect our choices under pressure; assuming that we have taken the time during the slow and steady 'barrack' time to understand Him closely.

PRAYER

Father God, help me to walk with You in the ordinary seasons of life, so that when I am on the frontline I will respond in an appropriate manner. Amen.

NOTES FROM THE FRONT

13 God's purpose

SARAH KOMEN

After finishing basic training in August 2005, my first posting was to Chippenham, Wiltshire. My husband and I experienced a lot of blessings during this posting, the most significant being the birth of our second son, Alfred. Our older son, Claude, was seven years old.

I transferred from the Royal Logistic Corps (RLC) to the Adjutant General's Corps (AGC). After my transfer course, we were posted to 1 Rifles in Chepstow. Two weeks after arriving at the new unit, I was unexpectedly deployed to Afghanistan at very short notice. This deployment was particularly difficult because Alfred was just sixteen months old when I left. My husband Theo is a great dad, and very involved with the children, but I hated having to miss both Claude and Alfred's first day at nursery and school. I also didn't have a chance to attend our new church before deploying. The love of Christ is such that the Christians at the new church prayed for us and supported my family and me, even though they had never met me.

The tour was very challenging. I wondered why I had ever joined the Army, and questioned why God would want me to work in such a costly way. While there, I determined that I would leave the Army so I could spend more time with my family. I even enrolled on a course to enable me to get a civilian job.

After deployment and the usual medal parades and leave, I resumed work. That is when I met a SASRA member who was speaking passionately to the soldiers about Jesus. He had the ability to stop the busy soldiers and in brief but powerful seconds, introduce Jesus to them. After breaking the ice, he would send them to my office. I would give them Bibles, invite them to lunch-time prayer meetings and to attend church. Suddenly, there was a buzz about Jesus. Some soldiers were curious, others were afraid and still others were sceptic. The OC even came in to ask what part Jesus played in the training plan.

It was at this point that I realised my purpose for being in the Army. Far from just being a means to earn a living, I was there for God's purpose. From then on, my attitude towards my job changed. I love it and I now know I am in the right place.

The dog ... madness by the world's standards!

66

WITH
Jos McCabe

Luke 11:1–10; Luke 18:1–8

So I say to you: ask and it will be given to you; seek and you will find; knock and the door will be opened to you. For everyone who asks receives; the one who seeks finds; and to the one who knocks, the door will be opened. **LUKE 11:9–10**

Fermanagh, Northern Ireland, c. 1979. Another border patrol ... long, tiring and dangerous. The Marines reached an isolated farmhouse, where they were greeted by a sudden yelp. Immediately they were on guard, a short run followed and there in the slurry pit was a dog struggling to get out. One brave young Marine did not hesitate; he dropped his weapon, took off his webbing and jumped in!

He did not know the depth or the danger but somehow he managed to get hold of the slippery dog and his oppos got him out. For the rest of the patrol his saturated kit smelt strongly and he was deeply uncomfortable but he had no regrets; he loved dogs and felt that he would have drowned if need be to save this one.

Jesus told a number of stories that displayed people acting in ways that were also 'madness' by the world's standards. The ones in today's readings are good examples. The corrupt judge in Luke 18, who thinks normally only of himself is provoked into uncharacteristic action by the widow-woman's persistence. Luke 11 tells of the resolute neighbour who makes such a nuisance of himself in the middle of the night banging on his neighbour's door, that his sleepy friend is forced into hospitable action. The point Jesus makes of all this shameless audacity is this: how much more will God who loves you and would do anything for you, to the point of dying for you, do for you if you ask Him? What is stopping you from asking Him today?

PRAYER

Lord Jesus, thank You that these stories show me that You love me and that You will hear me when I pray. Thank You that You demonstrated Your love for me in dying for me on the cross. Today I want to bring the following issues and situations to You ... Amen.

67

Anon

Confrontation with fear

Isaiah 41:8–16; 2 Timothy 1:3–7

So do not fear, for I am with you; do not be dismayed, for I am your God. I will strengthen you and help you; I will uphold you with my righteous right hand. **ISAIAH 41:10**

Towards the end of the conflict in Afghanistan, when casualty numbers were high, I fell into conversation with two officers serving in a brigade imminently deploying to theatre. 'The boys are tired,' one of them told me, 'they don't want to go back. They think they have been lucky so far, but those who are going out for their third or fourth time have a very real fear of coming back inside a body bag.'

I can understand the power of fear. It paralyses our thoughts and action. It kills morale. According to psychologists it even has a physiological effect on our body, causing, amongst other things, our heart to beat faster, increased sweating and changes to our digestion. Everyone feels fear at certain times in their lives, and it is often said that true courage is not the absence of fear but the willingness to bravely continue with a chosen course of action.

The Bible has a lot to say about fear. I have heard that there are 365 Bible verses relating directly or indirectly to fear. That is one for every day of the year! The passages in today's chosen readings illustrate two key biblical points about fear. The first is this; that fear does not come from God. Yes, it is a natural human response, but as John points out in 1 John 4:18, 'fear has to do with punishment'. God is a God of infinite and complete love; therefore there 'is no fear in love'. Writing to Timothy, Paul reinforces this, 'God has not given us a spirit of fear, but of power and of love and of a sound mind' (2 Tim. 1:7, NKJV). The second truth the Bible teaches us about fear is shown in Isaiah 41:10. It tells us that even though our fears are not of God, He understands them and more than that He promises to be with us and strengthen us during those times we are afraid.

PRAYER

Lord, I commit my fears to You. Amen.

Hospitality for the RN

68
WITH
Kevin Shaw

1 Peter 4:1–11; Matthew 25:34–46

The King will reply, 'Truly I tell you, whatever you did for one of the least of these brothers and sisters of mine, you did for me.' **MATTHEW 25:40**

In my opinion one of the great things about being a Christian in the Royal Navy is that we have contacts with Christians in almost every port that a warship can visit around the world. Hospitality is offered on the basis of a phone call or email; sometimes it can be a meal, sometimes people give a tour to show off their town, and certainly a ride to church on Sunday. It can be a great form of outreach to friends on board – this is what 'real' friends do to support each other. But I am usually humbled by the experience as I get looked after by people who are usually far worse off materially – but so much richer in faith and joy! I have never so enjoyed a bar of chocolate as when shared by one family as a treat in honour of my joining them for a meal. The Russian bar was cheap – full of fibre to bulk it up and almost grey in colour. But the occasion was full of laughter and love. I still warmly remember what a privilege and joy it was to share that chocolate.

Throughout the New Testament, followers of Christ are urged to practise hospitality. For some of us this does not come easily. This was true even in the Early Church. Peter chided some of the recipients of his letter to 'Offer hospitality to one another without grumbling' (1 Pet. 4:9). When we take people into our homes and show them love, we are not just blessing them, but actually serving Jesus himself. 'For I was hungry and you gave me something to eat, I was thirsty and you gave me something to drink, I was a stranger and you invited me in' (Matt. 25:35). There may even be an added blessing now. The writer of Hebrews tells us that in practising hospitality some people have even entertained angels without knowing it (Heb. 13:2)!

PRAYER

Lord, show me who to bless with my home, time and other resources. Make me generous in spirit. Amen.

69

Anon

Fashion sense

Job 31:1–34; Matthew 5:27–30

I made a covenant with my eyes not to look lustfully at a young woman. **JOB 31:1**

It had been another cold, dark night on an extended exercise in Poland. I shared the 436 armoured vehicle with my crew. They were long, boring nights for the guys, who would often wash, shave, eat and read. One morning I woke up to find an addition to the ops map board ... a picture of a very naked lady from one of the boy's porn mags! Wanting to confront the issue in a diplomatic way, I fashioned some underwear out of tissue paper for the poor girl, and stuck it on with blue-tack whilst they were sorting out the vehicle. Needless to say the lads did not appreciate my artwork, 'You have to take it off, Sir!' to which I replied, 'No, *you* have to take *her* off, boys! This is an ops room!' When I returned from breakfast she had disappeared, never to reappear again!

As soldiers for Christ we know that we live in a broken, hurting and fallen world. There are times when God calls us to confront the sin we see and times when He simply asks us to pray. When we confront the sin, we need to confront it in an attitude of love for the sinner, as this is the way that God confronts us. However, as today's readings show, God, while loving us completely, is uncompromising about our own sin and expects us to be too. Jesus says, 'If your right eye causes you to stumble, gouge it out and throw it away. It is better for you to lose one part of your body than for your whole body to be thrown into hell' (Matt. 5:29). We know that temptation becomes a sin in our mind long before we act on it. When asked, 'What is the difference between looking at a woman and looking at a woman lustfully?' I give the reply, 'The second look!' Job made a covenant with his eyes not to look lustfully. Are there practical steps you might take today to deal with your unruly thought-life in this area or any other?

PRAYER

Lord, please show me any areas of sin that
You want to deal with today. Amen.

One foot in the grave

70

Anon

Corinthians 15:1–58; Romans 6:1–14

For since death came through a man, the resurrection of the dead comes also through a man. For as in Adam all die, so in Christ all will be made alive. **1 CORINTHIANS 15:21–22**

Anyone who has spent time talking to soldiers will know that there is a certain black humour that abounds in the place of tragedy, enabling them to laugh in the face of death. This was recently epitomised in a photo on Facebook showing an amputee with a new prosthetic leg. On the back of the surviving limb, across the calf muscle was a new tattoo: a pointing hand drew attention to the prosthetic. Under it was the caption: 'one foot in the grave'. This brave young man jokes about the stark reality of his human mortality. It is a sobering reminder for us too, that one day all of us will die. As someone has said, 'the only certainty of life is death'.

As Christians, whilst we know that death is certain, there is hope. The reason for this hope is explained in detail in 1 Corinthians 15. It is based entirely on Jesus. Paul puts it like this, 'For as in Adam all die, so in Christ all will be made alive' (v22). Yes, we will die humanly speaking, but this is not the end; there is an eternal life to look forward to. Christ's resurrection is the guarantee that we have that this is so. Paul calls His resurrection the 'first fruits'. Right at the beginning of the summer, when a tree has a few early fruits, you can be sure that later on there will be a good harvest. It is the same with Jesus' resurrection. The eye-witness accounts of the truth of His rising from the dead give all of us hope; hope that can lead to the courage and humour shown by professional soldiers to laugh in the face of death. 'Where, O death, is your sting? (1 Cor. 15:55).

PRAYER

Lord, help me to fully grasp the reality of Your resurrection, so that I may live for Christ. Help me instead put to death the sin that so easily overwhelms me; remembering that I can live a new 'resurrected life' starting right now! Amen.

NOTES FROM THE FRONT

14 Was it an angel?

PHIL EXNER

I was brought up in a Christian Catholic home. My parents were sincere believers and taught me about God. However, there came a point in my life when I began to ask myself, 'Do I really believe? Is what I have been taught true?' I went through an extensive period of exploring everything from other religions to existentialism and post-modernism. At the same time, I continued to advance in my Christian knowledge in things like doctrine and dogma. My life was less than pure as I wrestled with the reality of faith, although externally I was still a 'good Christian', even a 'good Catholic'!

I started dating a girl shortly after becoming a pilot in the US Marine Core. However, we couldn't decide which church to go to. We thought it was important to go to church together but neither of us wanted to stop going to our own church. We decided that if we couldn't resolve this within a six-month period we should break up. After six months we were still at stalemate, so after a tearful goodbye she dropped me off at an airport where I boarded a plane for the first leg of a journey that would take me to my duty station.

As I sat on the plane, I questioned why I could turn away from a girl whose love was very real, for a God that I had once experienced, but to me really was little more than a concept.

The plane landed and I arrived at the internal check-in counter only to discover that my ticket had been mistakenly cancelled by the Air Force. The clerk suggested I buy another ticket, which could be refunded later. It was at this point that I realised I'd left my wallet in my girlfriend's car 400 miles away. I had nothing but small change in my pocket. Needing help, I put on my uniform and travelled out to a nearby Air Force base. I was able to get through the gate, but once inside no one would help a man without ID or a set of orders. Not knowing what to do, I sat on my bags in the huge space designed to ship entire battalions out to Vietnam. There were hundreds of people all scurrying around, but I was alone; away without leave and no one knew where I was. I was surrounded by all my worldly possessions and in my pocket I had a mere $1.20. Desperate, I began to pray, 'God, I don't know if You are real, or if I am talking to myself, but if You are trying to get my attention, You've got it. If You have a message or anything for me, I am ready to hear it.'

I looked up and at the far end of the terminal was a woman who looked as though she had been sleeping rough. She didn't fit in at all. I noticed that her eyes were locked on mine, and no matter who walked between us, her eyes never left mine. She walked right up to me as I sat with my luggage: 'Young man,' she said, 'I have a message for you from God ... stand up.' As I stood up she said, 'Hold out your hand.' I did so. Touching each finger she said slowly, 'I ... will ... never ... leave ... you – now you say it.' She made me repeat it a number of times. She said, 'That is from Hebrews 13:5, and also from Joshua 1:5. Never forget that, it's your answer.'

I was looking down at my fingers, and when I looked up she had disappeared back into the crowd. 'Wow,' I thought, 'If that is true then I am not alone.' So I got up and spent 92c on a super jumbo sized coke and lifted it up as I toasted the Lord. 'Well, here's to You Lord ... what are You going to do about *our* problem?' A moment later the assistant manager came over to me. 'Lieutenant, I have been looking for you all over.' Soon I was on my way. However, I have never forgotten that encounter with the lady or the message that God had for me that day.

Reduced readiness

71
WITH
Rich Anderson

Luke 12:35–48; Luke 21:25–36

You also must be ready, because the Son of Man will come at an hour when you do not expect him. **LUKE 12:40**

On a hot July day in 2009 in Helmand, where I was co-pilot on Chinook helicopters, I was fast asleep, catching up from an early start. Our captain, Mark, was also snoozing, sunbathing outside with his iPod on. When the 'shout' came, we all rushed out to start the cab, and waited – there was no sign of Mark. He didn't know we had had the shout and was still sunning himself! The other guys in the tent hadn't told him and I didn't know where he was when I had jumped up and run out of the door. We all thought someone else had told him!

In today's readings Jesus gives clear directions and instructions to His disciples on the importance of being ready for His return. As soldiers for Christ we need to live in a state of high readiness as if we were on 'ops', as we don't know when the final 'shout' will come. Jesus likens this readiness to the servants who would wait at the door to open it at their master's return. He says it will 'be good for those servants whose master finds them watching when he comes' (Luke 12:37). Furthermore, Jesus explains that there will not be any warning; He can return at any time. Christians in the past have overreacted to this command and lived as if it would certainly happen tomorrow; some have even sold up all they had in order to wait! I don't believe this kind of readiness is what Jesus means. Rather, like the guys and girls on the frontline, we also need to be in a state of readiness to spring into action as soon as the 'shout' comes. If we neglect the need to be careful, he warns that our 'hearts will be weighed down with carousing, drunkenness and the anxieties of life, and that day will close on you suddenly like a trap' (Luke 21:34).

Let's be alert and ready, even when we are sunbathing with our iPods on!

PRAYER

Lord, help me to live for You in everything I do, so that I am always ready for Your return. Amen.

72
WITH
Tim Symons

A culture of honour

1 Samuel 2:27–35; John 12:20–26

Therefore the LORD, the God of Israel, declares: 'I promised that members of your family would minister before me for ever.' But now the LORD declares: 'Far be it from me! Those who ***honour me I will honour****, but those who despise me will be disdained.'* **1 SAMUEL 2:30** (emphasis mine)

There is much being said in the Western Church at the moment about the importance of developing a culture of honour in which members of the church pay honour to, and respect, those who serve them. In the press there is a different message, where an 'honour culture' is the justification for revenge killings and other atrocities. Within the UK there is the biannual 'Honours List', which includes the names of servicemen and women who are singled out for their remarkable service for Queen and country. The Bible preaches a different message again. God promises to treat those who love Him and honour the Son, with honour in turn.

But what does it mean to honour God? For Tim Symons, serving in the Royal Artillery, it meant not playing sport on Sunday afternoons. 'At one stage in my career I played hockey and this led to me being asked to play for the Army. This was an honour, but before I accepted I said that I would like to play but could not be available for Sunday games because the travel involved meant that I would not be able to attend church. This limitation was graciously accepted and I was selected to play for the Army for Saturday games only, much to my delight. It was a case of "those who honour me I will honour"!'

The things in which God asks us to honour Him will probably differ for each of us, but they will all involve a choice between who has first place in our lives. Is it God or is it our own desires? Ask God to show you how to honour Him better today.

PRAYER

Lord Jesus, King of the universe, please show me if anything I am currently doing is not honouring to You. Please teach me how I should honour You and help me to honour You today, my King and my God. Amen.

Shadow of death

73
WITH
Nigel Watts

Psalm 23:1–6; Isaiah 41:8–13

Even though I walk through the darkest valley, I will fear no evil, for you are with me; your rod and your staff, they comfort me. **PSALM 23:4**

It took me a second to realise that if I had been driving along the road just a few minutes earlier I would have been killed! Every day we monitored where the attacks had taken place around Baghdad, especially along 'Route Irish', my drive to and from the city. On that particular day I glanced up to the digital map with the many red dots, indicating attack locations. I suddenly realised I have driven past one of those red dots just minutes earlier. On this daily commute there was nothing I could realistically do to stop being a target. After Gulf War 2, terrorists used to blow themselves up, normally in silver BMWs, taking as many of us with them as they could. I would travel daily between a secure location in downtown Baghdad and the airport, mid-morning and in the dead of night. On the morning commute we would be forced to join long traffic jams with other cars waiting to be cleared into the airport perimeter. It was a nervous time, our eyes darting around looking for suspicious people who might at any minute fire on us. During the dead of night trip back to Baghdad, after our operations, we would drive with no lights, as fast as we could, night vision goggles on, weapons ready and secure radios handy.

As the days turned to weeks, and more people lost their lives on this most dangerous of all roads in Iraq, the Lord impressed on my heart these wonderful words from Psalm 23, 'Even though I walk through the valley of the shadow of death, I will fear no evil, for you are with me' (Psa. 23:4, NIV 1984). It was a point of total surrender. My life was in His hands. It was then and it still is today.

PRAYER

Lord, thank You for the promises You make to me in Your Word. Strengthen me today and remove the fear I often have. Help me to trust that whether I live or die, my life is in Your hands. Amen.

74
WITH
Mark Leakey

Search and Rescue

Isaiah 46:3–11; Psalm 18:6–19

Even to your old age and grey hairs I am he, I am he who will sustain you. I have made you and I will carry you; I will sustain you and I will rescue you. **ISAIAH 46:4**

It is good to know that when a catastrophe happens there are people who are trained professionally to conduct search and rescue missions. Air Commodore Mark Leakey RAF (Retd) describes a time he had to be rescued: 'I was in the Falkland Islands, shortly after the war with Argentina. The engine of my Harrier failed on the approach to Port Stanley. In the nick of time I pulled the ejection seat handle; I still remember seeing the aircraft crash into the sea below me as I was rocketed away from disaster. Forty-five minutes later I was rescued by a Royal Navy helicopter.'

In today's reading the prophet Isaiah speaks God's words to His rebellious people, reminding them that although they are headed for a major catastrophe (exile in Babylon), He is the One who is always looking out for them. He reminds them that His desire is to carry them, sustain them and rescue them throughout every stage of their lives; despite the fact that they were heading for a catastrophe of their own making. Sometimes we also can be on catastrophic collision courses owing to various ungodly attitudes and habits. We might have to take drastic action and pull the ejection seat handle in order to survive. But, as Psalm 18 shows, this very action sends a SOS signal to the heart of God who, like the RN, is ready to pick us up out of the cold deep water. God's intention in rescuing us is to bring us closer into relationship with Him. For Mark, this episode marked the start of a long road of rediscovery of faith – a road he's still travelling.

PRAYER

Father God, thank You that You love me so much and that You always hear me when I cry for help. Please rescue me from the deep waters in which I am currently floundering and draw me into closer relationship with You. Amen.

Relationships

75

Anon

John 17:6–19; Hebrews 11:1–10

For he was looking forward to the city with foundations, whose architect and builder is God. **HEBREWS 11:10**

Whilst serving in Bosnia I was involved with some community support work, focused on homeless families who were living in the local school. Extended families of up to eleven people were living in tiny rooms, often four to a bed. On one of our visits and talking to these women and children, I became aware that they were of mixed origins, some Serb, some Croat and others Bosnian. How was it that they lived in harmony when the conflict was due to the very same ethnic divides? They explained that each of them had married a Croatian man, when the cultural and religious differences were insignificant. Once the fighting began, however, they were rejected by their own and left without identity. Their small community was the bond they shared and this gave them hope and a future.

Jesus too was rejected by His own, by His family, the Pharisees, by His disciples, and is often rejected by us now. However, He humbled Himself and was obedient, even to death on a cross. The key verse from Hebrews carries a clue about how this was possible – Jesus had a different perspective, He was looking forward to the future, not focusing on the present. As Christians, we too are called to be in this world but not of it, to hold our grip on earthly things lightly. Abraham in today's key verse did this by keeping his heavenly destination in mind. Like these Bosnians we can feel alienated from our society with beliefs and values that are different to worldly 'norms'. We need to find community with fellow believers who share the beliefs that we have. We also need to spend time reading God's Word in order to rely more fully on God for our hope in the life which is to come. It is encouraging that Jesus prayed for us to have the strength to do this during His time on earth.

PRAYER

Lord, help me to focus on You more fully, so that I can be in the world, but not 'of' the world. Amen.

NOTES FROM THE FRONT

15 CASEVAC

RICH ANDERSON

In July 2009, Rich Anderson was a co-pilot on Chinook helicopters flying Casualty Evacuation missions in Helmand Province, Afghanistan. An extract from his diary reads ...

Two nine liners (reports) came in at the same time. Rob (the pilot) got the intelligence. We lifted and held for a minute or two, before going in. Rob did a crazy jink in order to land. Landed in field, only saw people surrounding it when we were very late finals, they were well hidden. First casualty was suffering from shock. He was broken, came on crying and shaking uncontrollably. Our QRF14 are the SAS blokes, so one of the big guys just gave him a big bear hug all the way back to Bastion. Second casualty had been shot straight though the head, right between the eyes. Must have been a sniper, came on in a very bad way, missing half the back of his head. Medics have just told us (thirty–forty mins later) that he's subsequently died. Everyone shaken up, especially Anna. Sam had to wash the blood off his shirt. That's the second Brit death we've picked up today and 3rd KIA today in total. Rubbish. I wasn't really affected by what had happened until I saw Anna and Sam's faces when I shut the aircraft down and realised that it was a serious event, and it's made me think a lot more since I've landed. The guys on the ground were just wearing flip flops and shorts with body armour and helmets. Anna mentioned how young all the guys seemed. And who's going to remember them? They'll be a mention in tomorrow's news, but that's about it. What a waste.

Reading accounts like this one can be a distressing experience. It illuminates the realities of war and conflict; harsh reality, faced by so many servicemen and women in the defence of their nation. Grace Turner, author of *The King's Gold*, sometimes talks about a picture she once had while praying. She was walking around a large English country house, in which people were behaving as if they were on the set of *Downtown Abbey*; riding their lovely horses around the park and having tea on the lawn. Some way back from the house was the wall of the property. Here a bloody battle was taking place, and the enemy was fighting at close range with outnumbered, wounded and exhausted troops. The people in the house and garden were oblivious to, or possibly choosing to deliberately ignore, what was happening so close to them. It was a surreal situation, and yet for many of us in the Western Church, this is an accurate picture of the Church; a church which chooses to forget or ignore its baptismal exhortation to 'fight valiantly as disciples of Christ, against sin, the world and the devil'.[11]

Jesus came expressly to 'destroy the works of the devil' (1 John 3:8, NKJV). He 'disarmed the powers and authorities, [and] he made a public spectacle of them, triumphing over them by the cross' (Col. 2:15). However, if there was no requirement for the Church to be involved in any fighting, Paul would not have told all believers to dress spiritually as soldiers (Eph. 6:11–17). True, this metaphor has been used and abused by Christians throughout history. However, the fact remains that one of the callings a disciple of Jesus has is to take his or her part, through prayer and intercession, in the great war against evil and wickedness.

God promises that even though many people may forget the names and exploits of the servicemen and women who die so bravely on operations, He will never forget His spiritual children, those who willingly give their lives to His service (Isa. 49:15). In fact, those who stay faithful despite terrible persecution and martyrdom are promised front row seats in heaven, right under the altar of God (Rev. 6:9). Their lives, given bravely, are never wasted or forgotten.

Joining up

76
WITH
Jos McCabe

Romans 8:28–30; Philippians 1:3–11

And we know that in all things God works for the good of those who love him, who have been called according to his purpose. **ROMANS 8:28**

How do you know if is it right or not to join up? I grew up with a strong desire to join the Armed Forces, even though my family had no real connections with the military. It is often only as we look back that we can see God's hand on our life and certainly I have come to believe that my strong desire to join the Royal Marines was God-given and that it was a calling. God was the unseen hand, He prepared the way, helped me to get the qualifications and my family's support, saw me through the initial disappointment of the first interview failure and the final elation of success. He blessed me with a wife who followed me around and sacrificed a lot to support me. He kept me going for nearly thirty-three years to prepare me for what came next.

The passage from Romans from which today's key verse is drawn, touches on the difficult issues of predestination. How much of our lives happen by chance or our own design and how much of them are planned and ordered by God? Sometimes it is only in looking back that we can see the hand of God who works all things together for good. The modern truism 'God doesn't call the equipped, but equips the called', is echoed in Paul's writing to the Philippians, as he explains that God 'who began a good work in you will carry it on to completion until the day of Christ Jesus' (Phil. 1:6).

After a full career in the military, I can look back and realise that it was a 'calling' according to His (and not my) purposes. What about you? You may have felt a sure sense of God's call upon your life, or you may have no idea. The important thing in either case is to fix our eyes on Jesus and leave the detail work to Him.

PRAYER

Lord, show me more clearly Your hand on my life that I may serve You fully. Amen.

77

WITH

Martha Howell

Rear-guard, prayer-guard!

Philippians 4:4–7; Isaiah 26:1–8

You will keep in perfect peace all who trust in you, all whose thoughts are fixed on you! **ISAIAH 26:3 (NLT)**

Philippians 4:6–7 can be summed up like this: 'don't worry ... PRAY! His peace will guard your hearts and minds.' I experienced this practically when the submarine my husband commanded was 'presumed lost at sea' during an extended period of radio silence. Teams, both sea and air, were on standby for the launch of an international search and rescue. As the commander's wife, I was called into the naval ops room; this is a common practice in the South African Navy and I knew the wives well. Before I started contacting the families I prayed for the sub, 'Lord, please keep them safe and let them make their presence known.' Right then an amazing sense of calm and peace came upon me. The hive of activity in the ops room all around me seemed to be something that I had no part of any longer. My mind was freed of all the horrible images of everything that possibly could have gone wrong at sea.

Amazingly, contact was re-established only minutes before the sub would have been 'presumed sunk' and the search and rescue mission launched. Upon their safe arrival home, my husband told me of the strong sense of urgency he had felt to make contact right at that moment – hours earlier than he had originally planned to!

Without God, our natural instinct is to worry rather than to pray. Worrying about something wastes an incredible amount of time and energy, because it achieves nothing and only tires us out with its endless circles! How wonderful then, that instead of worrying, we can pray about the situation, however dreadful, and not only will God hear those prayers and act, but He will also give us the peace of mind to deal with the fallout.

PRAYER

In prayer today, bring to God any situation that has been troubling you and where you have been worrying about the outcome. As you do so, let 'the peace of God, which transcends all understanding ... guard your hearts and your minds in Christ Jesus' (Phil. 4:7).

'20 times round my beautiful body, go!'

78

Anon

1 Timothy 4:1–10; Matthew 6:23

physical training is of some value, but godliness has value for all things, holding promise for both the present life and the life to come. **1 TIMOTHY 4:8**

SAS selection tests the limits of human endurance capability. The course consists of several phases, starting with 'the hills', a four-week test of navigation and fitness. Later stages remain physically demanding but also increasingly require mental learning and application. On any course there are those who prepare assiduously for the first challenge, the physical element, and pass 'the hills' with relative ease, but who neglect to prepare for the mental challenges to come. They are quickly exposed and eliminated. Ex-SAS soldier Pete Scholey, author of *SAS Heroes: Remarkable Soldiers, Extraordinary Men* explains why: 'Many people fail because the mind gives in to protect the body. If you can overcome this, the body will go that little bit further than the mind expects.'[12]

Fitness, strength and endurance are prized within the military, often meaning the difference between life and death on operations. However, it is not the only thing, as the gentle teasing remark often used by physical training instructors contained in the title today highlights. Paul recognised this when he wrote to Timothy, 'physical training is of some value'. However, as the verse goes on, for the spiritual soldier, 'spiritual fitness' or godliness is of even greater importance. It has significance far beyond the present, even to the life to come. To be godly is to be Christlike. 'Little Christs' is the literal translation of the word 'Christian'. Godliness requires considered and deliberate investment on our part: 'Seek first his kingdom and his righteousness' says Jesus in Matthew 6:33. Godliness does not happen by accident, it happens as we choose Christ and His kingdom on a daily, hourly and even minute-by-minute basis.

PRAYER

Father God, may I not be obsessed with 'my beautiful body' – health, wealth and fitness – but devoted instead in the pursuit of You. May I reflect You each day in all the choices and plans I make, so that one day that I will be adequately prepared for the life that is to come. Amen.

79

Anon

Owning up

Matthew 6:12; 1 Samuel 15:1–24

But the LORD said to Samuel, 'Do not consider his appearance or his height, for I have rejected him. The LORD does not look at the things man looks at. Man looks at the outward appearance, but the LORD looks at the heart.' **1 SAMUEL 16:7 (NIV 1984)**

Whilst in command of both officers and men, I had one young officer posted to my unit who, while charming socially, turned out to be fundamentally flawed in character. Not long after arriving, we deployed on a low-level infantry exercise. Walking into his platoon harbour area to find out how his section patrols were going, the Sergeant Major and I found him fast asleep. When we asked for a report he proceeded to blame his section commanders. On subsequent exercises he became lost on a number of occasions and continued to consistently blame others, even when it was obvious he was at fault.

King Saul too, was a man who, while outwardly a worthy leader, was inwardly a coward. In today's reading God gave Saul a command which he chose to obey only partially, being afraid of the people's response. Later, when challenged by the prophet Samuel, he blamed the soldiers under his command (v15). While we might struggle to understand the reasons why God gave Saul an order that seems to have advocated genocide, we can see that Saul was wrong to blame others for his own decisions. It can be humiliating to our pride to accept fault, but often we don't realise that, as well as showing us up in a bad light, it causes great pain to those to whom we answer.

Like Samuel in chapter 15, verse 11, who was 'was angry, and ... cried out to the LORD all that night' on Saul's behalf, I struggled to do what was right, wanting to see the best in my young platoon commander. Eventually, for failing to take responsibility and fundamentally failing to live up to the Sandhurst motto of 'Serve to Lead', I felt unable to recommend him for promotion. God is looking for people after His own heart, not just those who look good on the outside. Where do you need to take more responsibility today?

PRAYER

Lord, please help me to own up when I am at fault. Amen.

Freedom of the city

80
WITH
Rhett Parkinson

Mark 11:22–33; Matthew 16:13–20

I will give you the keys of the kingdom of heaven; whatever you bind on earth will be bound in heaven, and whatever you loose on earth will be loosed in heaven. **MATTHEW 16:19**

When my regiment moved out of their barracks in Nienburg, Northern Germany, they were given the freedom of the city; an honour which involved a parade and an address by a member of parliament. This particular politician had well-known views advocating nuclear weapons and a local group of anti-nuclear activists decided to make use of the media interest and stage a protest. As the regiment formed up and stood to attention to listen to the speeches, the protesters unfurled banners and began blowing whistles and shouting loudly. The press cameras all turned in their direction and tension rose. I wondered what the outcome would be. The guard commander moved in a line of unarmed soldiers between those on parade and the protesters, and the police were called. I was expecting riot police, but a short while later two German polizei arrived on bicycles, clad in lycra! They walked down the line of the protesters with their hands held out, whereupon the protesters meekly surrendered their whistles. Reaching the end of the line, they remounted their bicycles and left. Rather sheepishly, the protesters, silently and half-heartedly waved their banners for another five minutes before packing up and going home.

The protesters recognised the authority of the policemen. On a human level they were just men in cycling shorts, but they represented all the power of the German Law and State. Many Christians often feel powerless as they see the devastating effects of evil, sin and suffering on the world around them. And yet, Jesus tells His followers that they have been given the keys to the kingdom – the symbol of the authority to act on Christ's behalf; an authority that is backed up by the full power and decrees of the State of heaven. Jesus said that Christians could speak to the mountain and it would obey them.

PRAYER

Lord, help me to believe without doubting, that when I pray my words are backed up by Your authority and power. Amen.

NOTES FROM THE FRONT

16 Protected

ANON

Sometimes it is easy to see God at work, but at other times we can be oblivious to the protection we have unknowingly received from Him. This was brought home to me during the 1991 Gulf War, where I spent time serving in an Air Defence Tornado Squadron whose role was to protect valuable allied assets in the Middle East. We were on a high readiness alert in the cockpit in case of an Iraqi attack or to replace one of the other airborne aircraft becoming unserviceable. So we sat for several hours in the cockpit with the canopy open, while the engineers stood around waiting to assist should we be ordered to get airborne.

On one occasion the engineers suddenly disappeared, and reliant only on our radios for communications we were not sure why.

When they returned we discovered that the airport had been the subject of a Scud-missile attack, in fact a large fragment of one of the Scuds had landed on the airfield only a short distance from where we were. All the time the attack had lasted, we had been completely oblivious to the danger we were in. Yet we were safe, protected even, but we had not realised we were in any danger.

At other times the danger we are in can be much more apparent. I personally experienced this happening at the beginning of the same tour in 1990. Tornados had originally been deployed from their base in Cyprus when the war started. Some weeks later I was part of a team that flew five new aircraft out from the UK to the Middle East to do an aircraft change-over. On our return journey we planned to fly non-stop from our base in Dhahran back to the UK, a complex ten-hour flight involving several air-to-air refuelling sessions.

Flights of this length were unusual, and one of my engines ran out of oil as I flew over Northern France, necessitating me shutting down the engine and making a 'Mayday' call. After a long delay and some heart-stopping moments, presumably as they tried to decide what to do with an armed military aircraft needing a considerable space in which to land, they gave me a slot at Paris's number two airport – Orly. I landed there safely and was rescued by an engineering team from the UK the following day. I am glad to know as a Christian that when I feel surrounded by danger and call out 'Mayday' to God, my call is always heard. More than that, I am grateful for the countless times God has protected me whether I have realised it or not.

Battle for a Christian life

81
WITH
Vicky Roberts

James 5:10–11; 1 Peter 3:14

But even if you should suffer for the sake of righteousness, you are blessed. AND DO NOT FEAR THEIR INTIMIDATION, AND DO NOT BE TROUBLED **1 PETER 3:14 (NASB)**

During my first posting, as a very junior troop commander, I was the only Christian, the only female, the only junior officer and I was completely untrained in the unit's specialisation; so to say that my credibility was sometimes in question is an understatement! However, I tried my hardest and hoped that as a result of perseverance and professionalism, things would improve. Whilst deployed on operations in the Balkans with this unit, I tried to dedicate one hour each night to a mini-break; through a combination of reading my Bible and doing cross-stitch I was able to take my mind off the daily 'grind' and to relax sufficiently to have renewed enthusiasm for the next day. Rather than do this in the isolation of my accommodation, I did so in the communal area where others were playing cards, watching TV or reading magazines. My Commanding Officer was clearly surprised by my choice of activities and advised me, most sincerely and authoritatively, to either continue in the privacy of my bed-space, or to choose hobbies more befitting of a junior army officer.

Whilst I now see that this man had my own interests at heart, what he failed to realise is that being a Christian is a fundamental part of who I am, and who God created me to be. I decided, against his advice, to continue my activities. It led to a degree of victimisation and ridicule, both of which the Bible warned us that we may face as a result of our faith. However, I'm sure that it also led to a few of the conversations I had about the depth and strength of my faith, as compared to 'notional believers'. In addition the verses from James 5 tell us that like the prophets of old, we are blessed when we persevere in difficult circumstances.

PRAYER

Lord, give me courage to stick at the things I know are right, despite what others think. I pray that as I do so for my faith to be effective and a witness for You. Amen.

82

Anon

Never give up!

2 Corinthians 1:3–11; Romans 8:18–27

We were under great pressure, far beyond our ability to endure, so that we despaired of life itself. Indeed, we felt we had received the sentence of death. But this happened that we might not rely on ourselves but on God **2 CORINTHIANS 1:8–9**

Serving in the Royal Navy has meant that I have many memories of rough seas and sickness experiences. When I was going through young officer training at sea, keeping watches on the bridge, I felt so queasy that every time I went onto the bridge wing to take visual fixes to plot on the ship's chart, I had to be sick at the same time – every six minutes for four hours! That all went roughly to plan until the ship changed course ... resulting in my having to excuse myself to change! Then there was the time that we were transiting home through the Med, about to have our early Christmas dinner. The weather was pretty bad, causing half of the place settings in the officers' wardroom to go flying. Formal Christmas dinner was abandoned. In fact, I had already abandoned it and was lying on my bunk practising dying! I asked one of the stewards if he would be so kind as to bring me some soup, which he duly did. Arriving with a big smile on his face, he passed me a bowl of broccoli and stilton soup – I had to make a quick dash for the 'heads'.

All suffering, even seasickness, reminds us how truly helpless we really are and how dependent on God we need to be. Paul and other members of the Early Church during the first century were persecuted for their faith and many suffered even to the point of death. Like the members of the Armed Forces today, they did not give up because it got hard. They too had a job to do. Too often though in my faith, I feel like giving up and find it hard to stick at it when times are tough. How good it is to have God's Spirit who 'helps us in our weakness'.

PRAYER

Lord, help me to persevere and stick with faith even when things are hard and others make it difficult for me. Amen.

Peace time

83

Anon

1 Timothy 2:1–7; Jeremiah 29:7

I urge, then, first of all, that petitions, prayers, intercession and thanksgiving be made for all people – for kings and all those in authority, that we may live peaceful and quiet lives in all godliness and holiness. **1 TIMOTHY 2:1–2**

We'd all like to believe that decisions to go to war are never taken lightly, and that the reason for the decision is ultimately to bring peace and stability for the populace. Certainly this seems to have been the motivation for Neville Chamberlain and the British Government in WW2. In his famous speech on 3 September 1939 he said, 'This morning the British Ambassador in Berlin handed the German Government a final note stating that unless we hear from them by 11 o'clock that they were prepared at once to withdraw their troops from Poland, a state of war would exist between us. I have to tell you now that no such undertaking has been received, and that consequently this country is at war with Germany. You can imagine what a bitter blow it is to me that all my long struggle to win peace has failed.'

The quest for peace is also a motivation for the solider of Christ. As Paul writes, it is the Christian's desire to live 'peaceful and quiet lives in all godliness and holiness'. However, just as in WW2 when there was a battle to fight first, there is often a battle that spiritual soldiers need to fight also. It is fought with the big guns of petition, prayer, intercession and thanksgiving to Almighty God on behalf of individuals and situations we are part of, but also for the kings and queens of this world and all earthly governmental systems. It is God's expressed desire that people should come to a saving knowledge of His love for them. Where governments and legislation would conspire to block the freedom of Christians to speak out and share this good news, it is up to God's people to take up the spiritual weaponry of prayer in order to bring this freedom and peace.

PRAYER

Spend some time praying today for all in authority. Pray also for those countries where Christians are persecuted and where people are not free to speak about Jesus.

84

Anon

Infantry 2Lt - Bosnia

Mark 6:30–44; Colossians 3:1–14

When Jesus landed and saw a large crowd, he had compassion on them, because they were like sheep without a shepherd. So he began teaching them many things. **MARK 6:34**

I remember a cold winter's day patrolling through Bugojno, near Gornji Vakuf-Uskoplje, past empty roofless homes, few people, no cars – snow-covered desolation. I recall the scene in monochrome, simple black and white; I don't know why. It was cold sitting in the turret of the Warrior, heading home to base, a routine trip … then out came the children, running; young, smiling, shouting, bright faces; happy to see us, jumping up to the side of the vehicle and causing us to stop. Why were they pleased? Despite the horrors of 'their war' we represented something that they rarely had – hope. And then as we stopped and handed out chocolate and sweets and we returned a smile to theirs – we showed compassion. Those children would be in their twenties now; I wonder whether they recall the soldiers' care. Did it make their day? Did it make a difference to their future? Compassion, hope and mercy; God's characteristics seen in a soldier's war.

Compassion is not necessarily the first quality that springs to mind when one is asked to list the characteristics of a soldier. But it is a vital one. It stirs the heart towards taking positive action. It is compassion that prevents needless atrocities. It is compassion that makes soldiers, sailors and airmen and women honourable. Jesus taught and then fed the crowd because He had compassion on them. His compassion resulted in merciful actions that gave hope and a future. Later, in Mark 10:14, Jesus treated the children in the same way saying, 'Let the little children come to me, and do not hinder them, for the kingdom of God belongs to such as these.' These kind-hearted qualities don't just happen; they require deliberate choices. Paul writes 'clothe yourselves with compassion, kindness, humility, gentleness and patience' (Col. 3:12). What are *you* wearing today?

PRAYER

Father God, please enable me to see others as You see them. I choose to put on Your compassion, kindness, humility, gentleness and patience with everyone I come into contact with today. In Jesus' name. Amen.

Word of command

85
WITH
Vicky Roberts

Matthew 8:5–13; Matthew 17:14–21

For I myself am a man under authority, with soldiers under me. I tell this one, 'Go,' and he goes; and that one, 'Come,' and he comes. I say to my servant, 'Do this,' and he does it. **MATTHEW 8:9**

Early on in my time as a squadron commander, I was amazed that shortly after voicing an idea I had had, it was implemented. This was even more surprising when it was simply an idea and I hadn't actually thought it through completely but was using one of my staff as a sounding board! After it happened once or twice, I realised I had to be careful to make it clear whether our discussion was based on a concept or whether it really was my direction and I wanted it to be implemented without further deliberation!

In today's reading we see the centurion who believed that Jesus could heal his servant even without actually visiting the house, but simply by 'saying the word'. He was a man who was used to having his every command instantly obeyed. When he saw Jesus he recognised a far greater authority. Understanding the nature of authority he (rightly) assumed that all Jesus had to do was speak the word of command. This often makes me think, 'Why do so many of us struggle to believe that Jesus' words can accomplish so much so easily?' Why do I pray sometimes with such low expectations that my prayers will be answered? After all, Genesis clearly tells us about how God created the universe and everything in it, by the command 'Let there be …' and everything happened accordingly. What then is there which is impossible for God?

Jesus told us that if we had a mustard seed's worth of faith in Him when we prayed, we too could give the word of command and the mountain would jump into the sea. The authority behind those prayers comes from the position we hold in Christ, just as my authority in my squadron came from the position I held.

PRAYER

Lord Jesus, help me to better comprehend Your absolute authority and to live out my life with complete faith in You. Amen.

NOTES FROM THE FRONT

17 Fasting

ANON

During the last five years of my military service, God led me to the discipline of fasting. I started with a day, moved to two days and then onto five days, all of which I found extremely hard. I had to choose a time when I was not expected to do any physical exercise. I'd read about someone who'd done twenty-nine, forty-day fasts and as I read it I knew God was calling me to do one. I prayed for five years that God would help me when the time came. Finally it happened. I was on resettlement leave and had anticipated doing this fast six months later. However, God spoke to me and told me to start immediately! This was to be a fast of everything but water. During the first twenty days I was really upbeat and excited about doing the fast; but the last twenty days I found particularly testing. In fact, someone suggested that by doing this fast I could die. Then my mother got very seriously ill and nearly died, and something else that I was organising completely failed. I felt that Satan was trying to stop me doing the fast and it felt as if my world was closing in on me. However, by God's grace, I was able to complete the forty days. I didn't die and neither did my mother, and even the event I had been organising went ahead in a different way and was very successful.

We see in Scripture that short fasts were part of the normal everyday life of the disciples. Jesus says to His followers '*when* you fast …' not '*if* you fast …' (Matt. 6:16, emphasis mine). This practice continued in the Early Church accompanied by earnest prayer; the church fasted in Acts 14:23, for example, before appointing elders for the churches. However, I think it is very important to have a sense of calling before you undertake an extended fast. We read in Matthew 4:1–2 that Jesus was led by the Holy Spirit into the desert, where He fasted for forty days before being tempted by the devil. During that time God used fasting to strengthen His spirit.

The reason I felt called to fast was that I had a vision for a ministry which I believed was of God and felt it needed to be underpinned by prayer and fasting. I sensed the call to fast was to deny myself, to surrender to God and allow Him to direct the paths of the ministry. This ministry has now been going for eleven years and is one which has brought hundreds to know Christ, has set many captives free and we have seen healing and deliverance beyond what we could ask or imagine. Matthew 23:12 says that 'those who exalt themselves will be humbled, and those who humble themselves will be exalted'. The forty-day fast, I believe, was about me surrendering my will to God and being humbled before Him. However, it has not stopped with that first forty days. I regularly have to fast in order to remain humble and seek God's will. I believe God honours our obedience to His command to fast and to pray, and as we do, it can have an impact on individual lives, on people-groups and nations.

I wonder, is God calling you to fast?

86

Anon

Too well camouflaged?

Matthew 5:13–16; Ephesians 4:25–32

You are the light of the world. A town built on a hill cannot be hidden. Neither do people light a lamp and put it under a bowl. Instead they put it on its stand, and it gives light to everyone in the house. In the same way, let your light shine before others, that they may see your good deeds and glorify your Father in heaven. **MATTHEW 5:14–16**

I was in a job that came with its own Land Rover, and with the Land Rover came a driver. He was one of the best and I really enjoyed the long journeys that we did together. We talked about everything and anything. After a while he said to me, 'Sir, it's a funny thing but when I am driving you I don't swear – but when I'm not I do it all the time.' I didn't know what to say so we probably made a joke about it and carried on with the conversation.

Although we can all fall into swearing and I was no exception, as a Christian I deliberately avoided it then (as I do now), trying to make a clean mouth a natural part of the Christian life. But I had no idea that this small Christian witness had any impact, until my driver mentioned it. Whether we intend it or not, people notice our behaviour. What we do and say, and how we do it, just can't be hidden. If you think your faith is well camouflaged in your daily life, you are probably wrong.

I wonder, what do people notice about you? Is it part of your Christian witness? If, as Paul instructs in Ephesians, we are doing all we can to please (rather than grieve) the Holy Spirit, we can be confident that we are shining brightly with the truth of the good news about God's kingdom. That truth causes others to question why we are different ... so we also need to be prepared to give them an answer when that happens, ideally one that is spoken with 'gentleness and respect' (1 Pet. 3:15).

PRAYER

Father, please keep reminding me that in everyday life I am representing You to other people, whether in word or action. Please help me to live in a way that brings You honour. Amen.

Yomping

87
WITH
Vicky Roberts

Isaiah 40:28–31; Hebrews 12:3

Even youths grow tired and weary, and young men stumble and fall; but those who hope in the LORD will renew their strength. They will soar on wings like eagles; they will run and not grow weary, they will walk and not be faint. **ISAIAH 40:30–31**

When I was in training, one of our earliest exercises consisted of navigating a route around Wales, over three days, carrying all our kit. Much of it was done overnight and, being Wales and an exercise, in the rain. One of our group was amazingly cheery and spent the whole time (or so it seemed) singing 'Zip-a-dee-doo-dah, dip-a-dee-day' over and over again. She was extremely fit, especially over mountains, and took it all in her stride. Although her singing was at times very frustrating, much of the time it kept us all going, knowing that someone could do it easily, even if we'd have been very tempted to give up had we been alone. Even the act of focusing on her distracted us from the pain and repetition of taking pace after pace uphill and never seeming to reach the summit.

My spiritual journey is similar; sometimes it feels like I go up and down mountainous paths in the rain, never reaching the end. Knowing that nothing is impossible for God, and that He promises to be with us everywhere, often helps me when I feel like I cannot carry on and am tempted to give up. 'Consider him,' writes the author of Hebrews (and paraphrased by me), 'who endured so much, so that you will not grow weary or faint-hearted.' Focusing on Him can be a great distraction from whatever problem I am facing, and allows me to see it through His eyes, rather than from my own perspective. He lifts me up, like wings on eagles, and helps me to carry on, whatever the situation.

PRAYER

Spend some time today reflecting again on all that Christ has done for you. Perhaps re-read one of the Gospel accounts of His crucifixion or write a list for yourself. As you do so, bring the areas where you are struggling before Him and ask for His help to get to the other side.

88
WITH
Rosie Leakey

The peace process

Psalm 34:4–14; Isaiah 26:1–15

Turn from evil and do good; seek peace and pursue it. **PSALM 34:14**

For many years I sought peace over the question of what would happen when we left the RAF; where would we live and what would we do? It was a concern and at times a conflict and a battle within me that caused worry. Being so involved with the RAF station and church life, we never seemed to have the time to be able to prepare and sort things out ahead of time; praying and seeking God's peace in and through it all was the only course of action left. We are told to 'seek peace and pursue it' (Psa. 34:14). God, in His mercy, gave me His peace when He showed me that my home is in *Him* and not bricks, and that *He* would provide for all our needs as we trusted in Him. God in His loving kindness and mercy was faithful; He provided peace in the uncertainty and finally a physical home when the time was right.

Peace is an inner state of contentment and rest, regardless of external circumstances. It is a highly desirable prize and despite being earnestly sought after in books, self-help programmes, music and exercise, it is often an elusive quality! True peace does not depend on the external; things like agreeable activities, enjoyable occasions or even on other people being 'nice to us'! Instead, it is built on a relationship with God. As Isaiah 26:3 says: 'You will keep in perfect peace those whose minds are steadfast, because they trust in you.' Peace is a by-product of our trust flowing from our relationship with God. God's very nature is one of peace – as seen in Jesus' title: Prince of Peace. This does not mean that we are not affected by the suffering and pain that human existence brings, but it does mean that when we are in relationship with Him we are held in a place of hope and comfort; the perfect antidote to all-consuming worry.

PRAYER

Lord, thank You for Your gift of peace. Please help me to pursue You wholeheartedly and trust You with all my needs, and as I do so, I pray for an increase in Your peace. Amen.

Shocking!

89
WITH
Rhett Parkinson

Proverbs 29:1–6; 1 Timothy 3:1–7

Evildoers are snared by their own sin, but the righteous shout for joy and are glad. **PROVERBS 29:6**

We were out on a night patrol during basic training. An hour earlier the heavens had opened and we were all soaking wet. As we crossed a field we came to an electric fence and immediately went into our obstacle crossing drill. The first few guys had rolled under the wire and shaken out on the far side when the radio operator took his turn. As he crawled under the fence the antenna touched the electric fence. Immediately bright blue sparks, each one accompanied by a loud 'crack', began arcing from his nose to the wet grass. Initially surprised, we all fell about laughing! Fortunately, for him, the platoon commander planted a size twelve boot in the middle of his back, thus breaking the circuit!

The writer of Hebrews says that sin 'easily entangles' (Heb. 12:1). There have been many times in my own life where I have become ensnared in the consequences of my own sin. Consequences that have sent electric shock waves arcing through my private and public life with painful results! Sadly in many of these instances too, I have not been the only casualty, others too have become enmeshed in the fallout from my sin. It is also true that the standard required for a leader is always higher than that needed for a follower. Paul gives this advice to all those who aspire to leadership within the Church: 'have a good reputation with outsiders, so that [you] will not fall into disgrace and into the devil's trap' (1 Tim. 3:7). It is for that reason that I have found it so important to make myself accountable to an older and wiser Christian; one who will not be afraid to warn me of the dangers that lie ahead, and where necessary will be able to employ a large size twelve. Who could provide that role for you?

PRAYER

Lord, show me where sin is becoming a snare in my own life, and set me free from it completely. Show me who I can become accountable to, and if there are others whom I could mentor. Amen.

90
WITH
Rhett Parkinson

Who's the boss?

James 1:5–8; 1 Kings 18:20–39

And Elijah came near to all the people and said, 'How long will you go limping between two different opinions? If the LORD is God, follow him; but if Baal, then follow him.' And the people did not answer him a word. **1 KINGS 18:21 (ESV)**

Whilst in Canada commanding an armoured engineer squadron, I landed in 'hot water' with the CO after my orders were countermanded. I had two engineer recce sergeants who were my 'eyes' and the technical engineer experts working in the recce group. The forthcoming operation was an advance that commenced with a river crossing using armoured bridge layers. I told my guys to look for a crossing either side of an existing bridge which had been 'blown up'. The OC of the recce group then told them they could only focus on another specific part of the river where, it turned out, there were no suitable crossing points. This resulted in a significant delay of well over an hour whilst other alternatives to cross the river were considered. Had the recce sergeants obeyed my original orders, the whole battle group would have been across in a matter of minutes.

In today's reading from 1 Kings 18, the people of God were swaying between two sets of orders. On the one hand they had decided to follow God and His commands, but more recently, under the example of their king, Ahab, they were devoted to the local pagan god – Baal. Confusion reigned. James describes a man in a similar situation as double-minded and indecisive like a wave that blows backwards and forwards. It is impossible for a person like this to show the way for others to follow Christ, or indeed to be a follower of Christ themselves. Around the time of Jesus there was a well-known Jewish idiom to describe those who were the disciples of a rabbi; the disciples were to follow their teacher so closely that they would be covered 'in the dust of the rabbi'. God desires disciples who will stick closely to Him and attune themselves to His directions.

PAUSE

Whose orders are you following? Are there changes that you need to make in order to follow God single-mindedly?

NOTES FROM THE FRONT

18 Post-traumatic growth

OLLY CHURCH

Smith Wigglesworth once said, 'Great faith is a product of great fights. Great testimonies are the outcome of great tests. Great triumphs can only come out of great trials.'[13] Olly Church's life is a testimony to this statement. He has had a number of close shaves with death. He recently spoke about two of them ...

'I deployed to Afghanistan as a team leader on the advisory team for the Afghan Reconnaissance Forces. With hindsight this was probably one of the most dangerous jobs in theatre. However, it was a fascinating job as I worked with the Afghan Army and got to see just how big a part their faith played in their lives. As you can imagine, there was a great need for cultural empathy and understanding.

'On 6 May 2010 (Election Day) we were out on a fairly routine patrol when we were ambushed. We returned fire and then patrolled down to a nearby village to talk with some of the elders. Shortly after we arrived one of the guys asked me what had happened to the water bottle on the side of my day-sack. I looked down and saw that there was a bullet hole through it! On later inspection I discovered that the machine gun round had travelled through the side of my rucksack and bounced off my back plate. I had been literally inches away from death. That brought things into fairly sharp focus!

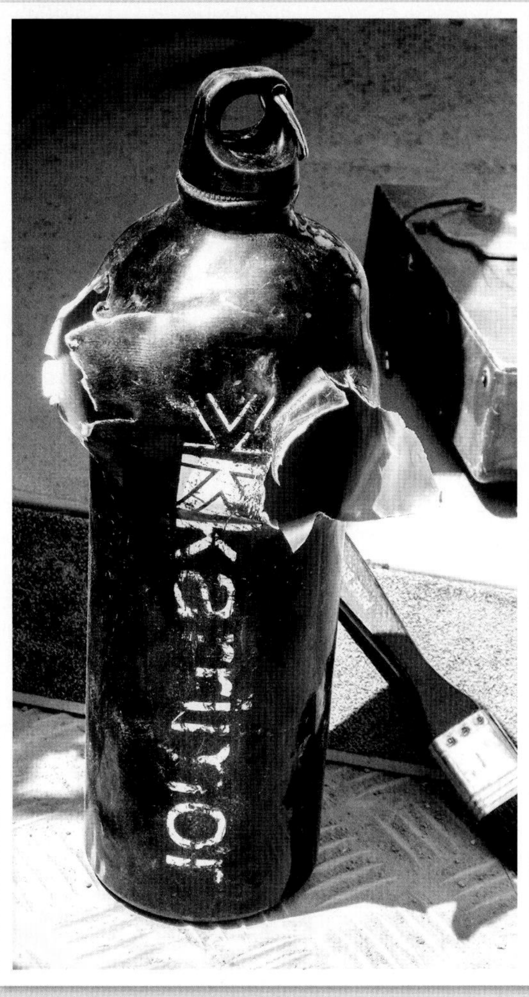

'Three days later, we were conducting another reconnaissance patrol into the green zone of the Helmand River when the 2IC of my team trod on an IED. It detonated and he was badly injured, losing a leg. We began to move him to evacuate him back to Bastion and I was actually warning the team not to step on a secondary device when I trod on one myself. I was extremely lucky; the device only partly detonated. However, although only the detonator exploded, it was still a high velocity shock wave. It shattered my heel into about nine pieces and also left me with some minor brain damage and other complications.

'It almost seems unreal looking back on it, but what it does do is it makes me realise how lucky I am compared to so many others who have lost one, two even three limbs. In some ways I am even thankful that this has happened. I appreciate that that sounds like an odd thing to say, and it does not mean that I have not had many dark days. I have. I do. However, what it has done is cause me to examine my life and make some big changes. If this had not happened, I expect I would have remained on the same trajectory. A lot has changed since it happened. I have left the Army and have formed a company with a friend, Simon, which seeks to use the skills and values of former servicemen to benefit society. We are making a lot of progress and it has helped me to realise that there can be post-traumatic growth. It has also required me to have faith in God. It is that which has helped me to get me through the dark days, as well as seeing how other people are often willing to give freely for something that is bigger to improve our community. And who knows, as Simon once said, commenting on the number of close calls to death I have had, perhaps doing this is one of the reasons why I am still alive.'

91
WITH
Paul Morris

Raw recruit

Romans 2:5–16; Isaiah 30:21

They show that the work of the law is written on their hearts, while their conscience also bears witness, and their conflicting thoughts accuse or even excuse them **ROMANS 2:15 (ESV)**

Towards the end of young officer training we had a presentation by the training wing OC on the subject of taking up new appointments. We were all very young and very keen to leave the training establishment and take up our first command. We had spent over a year training to be troop commanders and were excited at the prospect of getting on with our jobs in the 'real world'. This excitement was tinged, to a greater or lesser extent, with a fear of failure and the nagging question of whether we would be up to it. In my case I think this question loomed rather larger than for most. We were all young but I had joined straight from A levels and was, on completion of training, barely twenty. I had scarcely learnt the art of shaving, never mind leading Royal Marine Commandos! Something that the OC said at that briefing helped massively and has stuck with me ever since. He said that we were all clearly inexperienced but that we would *know the difference between right and wrong.*

The Bible backs this up. In Romans 2 Paul writes that our consciences are God-given instruments and that we are responsible for using them properly. Sometimes though, especially when we are new to faith, or have areas of our lives where we have been knowingly disobedient, the difference between right and wrong is not always clear. In those instances we need to pray that God will make it obvious in a 'This is the way, walk in it' manner (Isa. 30:21).

During the briefing the OC also told us to show moral courage and not close our eyes and ears to wrongdoing. We were to take active steps to do the right thing; not to walk on by. It is something that I have thought of often since and have tried to live by this simple, challenging but, in my experience, highly effective maxim.

PRAYER

Lord, refine my conscience today and speak to me clearly through Your Word. Amen.

Sacrifice

92

Anon

John 15:12–17; John 19:1–41

My command is this: Love each other as I have loved you. Greater love has no one than this; to lay down one's life for one's friends. **JOHN 15:12–13**

Paragraph 308 of the Sandhurst guide, *Developing Leaders*, states, 'The notion of service, not contract, must be at the heart of Army leadership. On joining the Army all personnel accept an open ended commitment of service and pledge to do their duties despite difficulties and dangers. This is expressed in the Oath of Allegiance in which all soldiers swear to subordinate their own interests to those of the Nation. At its extreme this might involve leaders giving their lives but more routinely placing the safety, security and needs of others before their own.'[14]

The many citations for posthumously awarded VCs are testimony to the fact that the military have been faithful over the years to live and die by this code. The ultimate model of a life lived for others is at the heart of the Christian faith. Jesus Himself lived and died not for Himself but for those He came to serve – us! He was motivated not by duty, but by love. Our extended reading today from John 19 provides an eyewitness account of the final few hours of His life. You might like to read and re-read this passage several times, asking God to speak to you in a new way as you do so. Jesus died so that we could have peace with God and live. He lived not for His own interests but for ours.

All British Army and RAF personnel are required to swear an Oath of Allegiance. No such demand is placed on Christians in a formalised manner. Instead, during baptism and confirmation Christians make public statements of belief before other believers and before God. Sometimes, I wonder what would our lives look like if we, like regular service personnel and reservists, pledged to subordinate *all* of our own interests; placing the needs of others, following Jesus and the extension of His kingdom, before our own desires and selfish ambitions … and really meant it!

PRAYER

Lord, too often I live for myself and not for You. Help me today to live for You and for others. Amen.

93
WITH
Andy McMahon

Safe ground

Psalm 121:1–8; 1 Samuel 2:1–10

He will not let your foot slip – he who watches over you will not slumber **PSALM 121:3**

During 2009 I was on patrol when our metal detector stopped working. Ever aware of IEDs, team morale suddenly plummeted. My 2IC staunchly announced that he would lead the patrol, but I told everyone to follow me – but a bit further back than normal! As I put each foot forward, I remember praying, 'This is over to You Lord. Please keep my feet on safe ground.' We proceeded safely, but not without a few prayers of gratitude!

As we came off the overwatch position, the lead scout was faced with two options to re-join the main track: left or right. He chose the right. As my foot hit the main track, the rest of the company was ambushed just fifty metres away, where we could have been had we gone left. Once again, I saw God's hand was upon us – and our company. Two RPGs and heavy small arms fire plunged into my colleagues at short range, with no casualties! As my team were outside the ambush, we put heavy ordnance onto the enemy positions and called in attack helicopters, which resolved the conflict in short order!

A few weeks later I was in church with my wife, we were singing Psalm 121. When I came to verse three I was overcome with emotion as the reality of the verse struck me, 'He will not let your foot slip'. I had seen 'close up' God's protection and care. The reading from 1 Samuel contains a similar sentiment, verse 9 says God 'will guard the feet of his faithful servants'. Throughout it all I am reminded that it is 'not by strength that one prevails' (1 Sam. 2:9). In other words, my safety during what was a frenetic dangerous tour was not the result of my choices and abilities but because the sovereign will of God who determines the length of my days had decided that my time had not come. Instead, He used the danger of my immediate environment to focus my attention on His Word and keep me in regular 'comms' with Him.

PAUSE

Spend some time reflecting on God's protection.

Word of command

94
WITH
Andy Smith

Mark 13:32–37; Acts 9:32–43

'Aeneas,' Peter said to him, 'Jesus Christ heals you. Get up and roll up your mat.' Immediately Aeneas got up. **ACTS 9:34**

In 2002 I commanded the Allied Company for a short period in Mitrovica; under the control of the French. It was a challenging time; our French colleagues had a difficult situation to police. On one occasion we provided security for the Commander of Kosovo Force (KFOR) General Marcel Valentin, a French General. I was escorting the General to visit one of my patrols when, as we approached the city centre, the traffic ground to a halt. Several hundred angry Serb protesters were blocking the main high street. General Valentin and I dismounted and approached the protesters. His bodyguards became increasingly twitchy, but the General was in no mood for tip-toeing around. The dispute involved a routine vehicle stop by one of my section commanders. The vehicle owner was complaining that the French soldiers never stopped him. The General was magnificent; in a whisper he asked what my intention was. I replied that we were here to enforce the rule of law; my commander had a legitimate reason to stop and search the vehicle and that we should stay until the job was done. With that the General looked the chief trouble-maker in the eye and said that this soldier worked for the French KFOR Commander and he had his orders to do his job and he would do his job here!

In today's reading from Mark, Jesus likens the period between His ascension until His return to that of a man going on a long journey. Before He leaves He gathers His servants and puts them in charge of all His affairs. He delegates His authority to them to act as His agents. In Acts we see Peter healing the sick and raising the dead in the name and authority of Jesus. These are not just empty words; God ensures that they are fulfilled. As Christ's representatives on earth we have His authority to carry out His commands and instructions.

PRAYER

Lord, may I be bold in prayer, recognising that You have given me Your authority to act as Your agent here on earth. Amen.

95
WITH
Vicky Roberts

The loneliness of command

John 15:1–17; Proverbs 18:24

I no longer call you servants, because a servant does not know his master's business. Instead, I have called you friends, for everything that I learned from my Father I have made known to you. **JOHN 15:15**

In the Royal Navy there is a phrase 'the loneliness of command'; describing how a leader must keep his or her own counsel, masking individual fears and doubts in order to maintain a position of authority. For myself, even in the Army, there were times during my sub-unit command when I felt quite lonely. My troops were a great bunch of people and we had a good balance of work and play in the 'office', including a fair amount of friendly banter, but due to my position I couldn't really be pals with them. My fellow officers were OK as colleagues but I didn't really have any friends amongst them either; often being the only female and the only Christian within a unit hasn't helped much either. There is a deep longing within the human psyche for a 'friend who sticks closer than a brother' (Prov. 18:24), someone who will be there for them whatever the external circumstances. Sometimes that friendship is found in marriage or with a friend of long standing. But even then, the nature of military life can mean there are long periods when we find ourselves alone.

The same can be true within Christian leadership where the pressures and responsibilities insulate us from others around us. How amazing then to read in John 15:15 that God, the Creator of the universe and everything in it, wants to call each of us His friends. What a privilege and honour to be able to approach the throne of the King of kings and Lord of lords directly, to tell Him our deepest concerns and to find comfort and peace from His Holy Spirit, who promises to be with us always.

PRAYER

Thank You Lord Jesus for the friendship You offer me.
I choose to come to You today with these issues and
concerns (spend some time telling Him about them in order
to receive His wisdom, comfort and peace). Amen.

NOTES FROM THE FRONT

19 Quick response

ANDREW MCMAHON

God has been amazingly gracious to me during my time on operations in providing me with Christian fellowship. However, in 2009, when I was deployed to Kajaki, I dragged my heels for a bit and didn't actively pray that God would provide another believer with whom I could spend time. I realised that I needed to repent of my own passive attitude and went outside of my accommodation to pray. I sat in the shade of the parachute silk, looking out over the whole area we were operating in; it was very peaceful. After praying I felt incredibly relieved, having cast my burdens on God and after a few moments of reflection I picked up a book and started to read.

Before I had read even a page I thought I heard something not unlike gospel music. I remember looking at the sky and thinking, 'It will be a bit too much Lord if this is angels singing!' I looked up; there was no one in sight but the sound seemed to be coming from my right. This was bizarre because the building standing there belonged to the Mortar Section, and they had a reputation of being a wild-living bunch! I had to investigate, and as I stepped into the dusty room I said, 'Fellas, this is probably going to freak you out, but I can hear something that sounds like gospel music coming from this building.' Without even looking up from the card game one of the guys said 'Oh yes, Boss, that's the Fijian lads. They get up early every morning to pray, and they say grace at every meal. They are always listening to gospel music – just go on through.'

As I entered the small room at the back it was like entering a chapel, as the near wall was covered with scripture texts, prayers and a few drawings of rifles which dominated the space. It also contained two small bunk beds and two stocky well-built Fijians who had their Bibles open. The gospel music I had heard was pouring from their iPod. These two guys, 'Cam' and 'V', became God's answer to my prayers for fellowship. Each morning we would meet at half past six to pray together. We didn't just pray together but we also worked together, dropping our mortars, rockets and bombs onto the insurgents. This is an especially poignant memory for me, realising that no sooner had I asked God for fellowship than He provided it and it was just on the other side of the wall!

Seasick!

96

Anon

James 1:2–4; 1 Thessalonians 5:16–18

Rejoice always, pray continually, give thanks in all circumstances
1 THESSALONIANS 5:16–18

Have you ever made the short ferry crossing from Dover to Calais in rough seas, one which left you feeling a bit queasy, counting the minutes until you stepped back on to firm land? If so, imagine how you might feel if you were stuck in a tin can in the North Sea during February as part of the annual multinational Joint Maritime Course for ten days; regularly in gale force 8–10, in a cabin just aft of the fo'c'sle and exposed to the elements with the huge waves crashing next to your head as you try to sleep! Or, imagine swirling around like you're in a blender for forty-eight hours while passaging through the Bay of Biscay with its infamous swells, or jarring your legs as you swing down bleary eyed out of your bunk in the Irish Sea in gale force 7, only for the deck to make contact with you at the wrong time – a bad start to the day!

How does one cope with such 'momentary' trials and tribulations? I have tried lots of different ways. The most memorable was the time when the best thing I could eat were 'happy face' biscuits despite feeling decidedly unhappy! Another time it was fruit pastilles ... until I ran out! I have even tried lying down on my cabin floor and praying for the rapture to come, or at least for the Lord to make an exception for me, like Elijah, and let me go to heaven early!

Rather unhelpfully in my opinion, James begins his letter telling believers to consider it 'pure joy' when they face trials of many kinds. Why? Because trials develop our character and make it stronger. What trials are you currently facing? Fruit pastilles or happy face biscuits won't work, but 'thanksgiving' really does. Try it today!

PRAYER

Lord, help me to face the situation I find myself in currently with Your grace and fortitude, and to give thanks in all circumstances, knowing that You are developing my faith and my character into Your likeness. Amen.

97

WITH

Rich Anderson

'Hit' by enemy fire

Psalm 56:1–13; 1 John 5:1–5

for everyone born of God overcomes the world. This is the victory that has overcome the world, even our faith. Who is it that overcomes the world? Only the one who believes that Jesus is the Son of God. **1 JOHN 5:4–5**

The day of 25 July 2009 started off like any other, flying Chinooks on ops in Helmand. We crossed over a number of compounds and then we felt a slight jolt through the airframe. No one said anything at first until Dom said he thought he'd felt something pass through the airframe. I checked the temperature and pressure, but couldn't find anything. We were carrying a 4.5T Under Slung Load and didn't make much of it, thinking we'd check for holes when we got on the ground, so we continued our mission. We dropped the load and carried on to pick up people. When we finally got back to Bastion and were refuelling, Dunk said he'd go to look for holes. He found one so we shut down; damage from two rounds, including one in the nose box, was discovered. The engineer said it should have ripped itself to pieces. Somehow it had kept on working! Had we lost our engine, we would have been over Kajaki Lake and it's likely that we would have had to ditch into the water with very little chance of survival – it's not easy to swim with body armour on!

Christians are warned that that they are the target of the 'flaming arrows of the evil one' (Eph. 6:16). Sometimes these attacks come through physical events, but sometimes, as the psalmist describes, they can come through the people we live and work with. In all these events the victory comes when we put our faith in God, who made us. He alone is mighty to save, protecting us, so that even on those occasions when the round pierces our spiritual and emotional armour, we can walk away to fight another day.

PRAYER

Lord Jesus, I choose You again today as the source of my faith. I put my trust in 'God, whose word I praise – in God I trust and am not afraid' (Psa. 56:4). Amen.

It takes more than one to form an army

98

WITH

Ben Campbell Colquhoun

Romans 12:3–8; Ephesians 2:19–22

in Christ we, though many, form one body, and each member belongs to all the others. **ROMANS 12:5**

Throughout my military career I have discovered that God uses people. For a while I was in a job which took me in and out of Afghanistan quite regularly. On the two visits where I also bounced up from Helmand to Kabul, I discovered in surprise that the pilot of the C130 was a fellow Christian whom I knew from the Armed Forces' Christian Union. We were able to encourage and pray for each other. The odds of that happening were extremely slender; that we would both be out there at the same time on each occasion, and that his crew would be on that flight. This was very much a 'godly coincidence' and was a huge blessing to me during a stressful time.

I find that modern evangelicalism in the West often has a very singular focus – 'How is it for me?' The emphasis is on 'my' church, 'my' faith, 'my' journey. This is compounded by the fact that being a 'lone' Christian without a church family is relatively easy today, as so much excellent material is accessible electronically. This is not necessarily a bad thing; however, it is in contrast to the biblical picture which is one of corporate worship and experience. Paul describes this as 'one body'. Equally, the Armed Forces are corporate bodies consisting of lots of people; individuals working together to achieve the same goal. Many Christians describe feeling like 'lone soldiers on patrol', even though in the real Army this *never* happens. Even snipers work in pairs. As today's readings show us, the isolation that Christians can feel is contrary to the will of God who desires to use other people to support and encourage us as we support and encourage them. Who are the fellow 'warriors' with whom God wants to surround you? Ask Him to show you today.

PRAYER

Lord of heaven's armies, I pray that You will break down the walls of self-sufficiency in my life. Help me to see my role in Your army and the fellow troops who surround me. Amen.

99
WITH
Rhett Parkinson

Commissioned

Matthew 28:16–20; Luke 24:44–49

Therefore go and make disciples of all nations, baptising them in the name of the Father and of the Son and of the Holy Spirit, and teaching them to obey everything I have commanded you. **MATTHEW 28:19–20**

When I was commissioned into the Army I, like every officer, received a signed copy of the Queen's Commission. It reads:

To Our Trusty and well beloved Rhett Ian Brian Parkinson. Greeting.

'We, reposing especial Trust and Confidence in your Loyalty, Courage, and good Conduct do by these Presents, Constitute and Appoint you to be an Officer in Our Land Forces from the Eleventh day of December 1993. You are therefore carefully and diligently to discharge your Duty as such in the Rank of Second Lieutenant or in such other Rank as we may from time to time hereafter be pleased to promote or appoint you to, of which a notification will be made in the London Gazette, or in such other manner as may for the time being prescribed by Us in Council, and you are in such manner and on such occasions as may be prescribed by Us to exercise and well discipline in their duties such officers, men and women as may be placed under your orders from time to time and use your best endeavours to keep them in good order and discipline. And We do hereby Command them to Obey you as their superior Officer, and you to observe and follow such Orders and Directions as from time to time you shall receive from Us, or any your superior Officer; according to the Rules and Discipline of War; in pursuance of the Trust hereby repose in you.'

As followers of the King of kings, our Lord Jesus Christ, we have an even greater commission and one which carries far greater authority and responsibility. God has entrusted us with following His commands. There is no Plan B – we are the ones God has put His faith and trust in to get the job done.

PAUSE

Re-read the Bible readings and Queen's Commission prayerfully, asking King Jesus to show you how He has placed His trust in you and commissioned you to follow His commands.

'Roger – Out'

100
WITH
Tim Symonds

Hebrews 1:1–4, 4:12–13; 2 Peter 1:12–21

For the word of God is alive and active. Sharper than any double-edged sword, it penetrates even to dividing soul and spirit, joints and marrow; it judges the thoughts and attitudes of the heart. **HEBREWS 4:12**

As a Christian in the Royal Artillery, thoughts of going into full-time Christian service often crossed my mind and became a matter I prayed about. One day I saw a flyer about vacancies at the MOD Chinese Language School in Hong Kong, to learn Cantonese. The idea appealed, so I prayerfully applied and was granted a place following completion of my next posting. I eventually arrived in Hong Kong and started the two-and-a-half-year language course. I was reading my Bible one morning, not long after starting the course, when the words leapt from the page; 'Be strong and courageous and do the work ... the LORD God, my God, is with you. He will not fail you or forsake you until all the work for the temple of the LORD God is finished' (1 Chron. 28:20). I understood from this that learning Cantonese would not just be for now, but God would also use it in the future, which I found exciting. There was a time bar attached to the language course but, in time, I left the Army and returned to Hong Kong as a missionary, where I served for fourteen years with OMF International.

I love God's economy; nothing we do is ever wasted by Him. But even more than that, I love the fact that God delights to speak to us through His Word. For many believers this is the primary way in which God speaks. Hebrews 1:1–2 says ... 'In the past God spoke ... through the prophets at many times and in various ways, but in these last days he has spoken to us by his Son.' The words Jesus spoke are recorded in the Bible, as are all the things He has said through others under the inspiration of His Spirit. As we finish this study but continue to read the Bible, the same Holy Spirit inspires us and brings it alive in our hearts.

PRAYER

Lord, I pray that You would speak to me through Your Word about everything You have planned for me. Amen.

NOTES FROM THE FRONT

20 Quarter nightmare

ANON

We were familiar with the routine of moving and making the most of whatever house was allocated to us. The new quarter felt cold and dark and, although we tried to alleviate this with lamps, we couldn't seem to shift the atmosphere. Then we discovered that graffiti had been painted across the wall in a storeroom in big black letters. As time passed we realised that the sinister mood in the house was having a profound effect on the whole family.

At work, I suddenly found that I had lost all confidence in myself. I was at a loss to understand this, especially as I had recently been promoted and was doing a job I loved and felt equipped to do. At home, my wife began to experience strong feelings of fear. This was accompanied by depression and fatigue, leading to genuine illness and even a sense of death being nearby.

The children also subconsciously picked up on the atmosphere in the home. Our four-year-old daughter began having terrifying nightmares. One night she rushed in describing a 'scary man' chasing her. Around this time, my eight-year-old son returned home from school with a picture that he had drawn. As my son was not very good at drawing at the time, this picture was remarkable for its vivid details depicting very unpleasant images of children being harmed. We learnt that previous tenants had experienced a terrible tragedy in which a child had died. These experiences added to the fear my wife was feeling and made us suspect that there was some kind of ungodly presence in the house.

We decided that we needed to take action, although this kind of experience was new to us. The Bible tells us that Jesus won the victory over all the powers of darkness when He died on the cross (Col. 2:15). Furthermore, we saw that Jesus has given *all* His followers His authority over all the powers of darkness (Mark 16:17). God graciously provided us with some Christian friends who encouraged us to pray through the house, taking authority in Jesus' name over every ungodly presence that sought to steal, kill and destroy, especially the spirit of death. In 2 Chronicles 7:14 it says that 'If my people, who are called by my name, will humble themselves and pray and seek my face and turn from their wicked ways, then will I hear from heaven and will forgive their sin and will heal their land.' We wanted God to heal our land! So, we sought God's forgiveness for any sin that had been knowingly or unknowingly committed in the house, in the same way that Nehemiah did in Nehemiah 1:6. We commanded 'all spirits of death' to leave us and the house, in the name of Jesus.

We learnt about the power of praise and worship to cleanse spiritually. My wife is a gifted dancer and each day she would dance to praise and worship music in the room that had contained the graffiti, which we had also re-painted. We discovered that praising God in this way is a powerful weapon.

We saw that in spiritual battles of this sort the enemy often overplays his hand. These incidents and experiences were so compelling that they drew us together spiritually as a couple and brought me to my knees as I realised that God had given me His authority to pray for my family and fight for them.

God brought complete victory. The feeling in the house changed and my daughter's nightmares stopped. After we moved out the new tenants grew in faith and the wife began attending a Christian ladies' group. They were replaced with another Christian family – quite incredible as there are not *that* many Christians in the Army! Even more amazingly, we discovered later that, at the same time that we had prayed over the house, miles away in another country the previous tenant who had experienced the terrible tragedy involving the death of her child, conceived and went on to have a healthy baby. While in no way did this replace the child who had died, this joy brought healing and happiness to their family. God is so good.

Since then we make it a matter of routine to pray over each house in which we live, asking God to fill the house with His Holy Spirit and cleanse it from anything ungodly.

Endnotes

[Foreword]

1. C.H. Spurgeon, *The Soul Winner* (Grand Rapids, Michigan: Wm. B Eerdmans Publishing Co, 1963) p203
2. John Bunyan, *The Pilgrim's Progress* (public domain)

1. William Barclay, as quoted in Floyd McClung, *You See Bones, I See An Army* (Eastbourne: David C Cook, Kingsway Communications Ltd 2007) p31
2. Nicky Gumbel, *Bible in One Year* (London: Hodder & Stoughton, 2011) 28.9.2013
3. Some of this text first appeared in a SASRA magazine
4. leadershipgems.com/index.html
5. Definition of 'discipline' taken from *Concise Oxford English Dictionary* (Oxford: OUP, 2004) p408
6. *Worse Things Happen At Sea*, a light-hearted look at Clive Langmead's family life afloat in MV *Doulos*, is still available through online second-hand book stores.
7. The staff in the Armed Forces' Christian Union will be happy to provide help, if you would like it. Serving members of HM Forces may alternatively wish to speak to a Scripture Reader. Scripture Readers are evangelists who have a specific ministry to serving Army and RAF personnel. They operate in many Army barracks and RAF stations. They are employed by SASRA (Soldiers' and Airmen's Scripture Readers Association)
8. A fuller version of this story featured in *Contact* Magazine Summer 2012, see Jonny Palmer's blog: Living Life Risking
9. This paragraph first appeared in *Contact* Magazine Winter 2007
10. To find out more about New Wine, an annual Christian conference, visit www.new-wine.org
11. *Baptism and Confirmation – Church of England – The Liturgy of Baptism* (London: Church House Publishing, 2000) p68
12. Online interview with Pete Scholey www.ospreysas.com/qa.php
13. Julian Wilson, *Wigglesworth: The complete story: a new biography on the apostle of faith* (Milton Keynes: Authentic Media, reprint edition 2011) p108
14. *Developing Leaders. A Sandhurst Guide* Pilot version Easter 2012 (Crown Copyright MOD 2012) p23

List of contributors

Flt Lt R Anderson RAF
Rev JR Backhouse RN
Rev C Callanan CF RAChD
Lt Col BHG Campbell Colquhoun RE
Lt Col MT Cansdale MBE PARA
Capt (Retd) ON Church QRL
SSgt (Retd) J Crompton
Col (USA, Retd) P Exner
Mrs B Fishback
LTC (USA, Retd) J Fishback
Lt Col MP Goodwin-Hudson RHG/D
Lt Col (Retd) VH Hall OBE AGC(ETS)
Wg Cdr S Hayler RAF
Mrs M Howell
Cdr NK Howell SAN, SSK Sqn
Lt Col (Retd) C Kirke PhD RA
Cpl S Komen AGC(SPS)
Lt Cdr CF Langmead QVRM RD RNR
Air Cdre MA Leakey RAF (Retd)
Mrs RE Leakey
Maj SP Maggs QRH
Rev CA Maynard CF RAChD
Major AJ McMahon RA
Col (Retd) J McCabe OBE RM
Lt Col PEM Morris RM
Flt Lt JP Palmer RAF
Maj (Retd) RIB Parkinson RE
Capt (Retd) EM Rathbone RLC
Lt Col VJ Roberts RE
Lt Cdr KLH Samuel RN (Retd)
Capt KNG Shaw RN
Col AG Smith late PWRR
Capt (Retd) GTC Symonds RA
Lt Col (Retd) NJI Watts AAC
A/Capt (Retd) PM Welland 5RR (Rhodesia)

Glossary of military terms

- **2IC** – Second in command
- **84MM** – The 84mm was a Carl Gustav antitank rocket launcher
- **AFCU** – Armed Forces' Christian Union – a tri-service, all-ranks, UK military Christian fellowship. With its roots in the Army Prayer Union, established in 1851, the AFCU is primarily a prayer union that exists to support its members in prayer and to provide opportunities for fellowship
- **BERGEN** – military rucksack
- **CASEVAC** – Casualty Evacuation
- **CO** – Commanding Officer of a battalion/regiment or station
- **DPM** – Disruptive Pattern Material
- **DRAG** – Central passage through the ship
- **EXERCISE** – military deployment for training purposes
- **FOB** – Forward Operating Base
- **HEADS (ON A SHIP)** – The ship toilets
- **HQ** – Headquarters
- **IED** – improvised explosive device
- **IFOR** – Implementation Force, run by NATO
- **JNCO** – Junior Non-Comissioned Officers
- **KINETIC** – slang used to describe dangerous operational tour characterised by frenetic activity
- **LMEM** – Leading Marine Engineering Mechanic
- **MAGAZINE** – Ammunition storage and feeding device
- **MARRIED QUARTER (MQ, QUARTER)** – a house or flat provided by the military for married personnel
- **MESS** – accommodation and dining facilities for different ranks (eg officers' mess, junior ranks' mess)
- **MOD** – Ministry of Defence
- **MOD 90** – ID cards
- **NATO** – North Atlantic Treaty Organisation
- **NEAR-PEER ENEMY** – an opponent with similar military might
- **OC** – Officer Commanding – army position usually held by a major in charge of a company or squadron
- **OP/OPS** – slang for operation

- **OP TOUR –** operational deployment usually lasting six months but can extend to a year
- **OPPO –** colleague; from the naval slang for opposite number, the person doing the same job as you on another watch.
- **PADRE –** term used for military chaplain
- **PIFWC –** Person Indicted For War Crimes
- **QRF –** Quick Reaction Force
- **RAF –** Royal Air Force
- **RMAS –** Royal Military Academy Sandhurst
- **RPG –** rocket propelled grenade
- **RECCE –** reconnaissance mission
- **SAS –** Special Air Service
- **SASRA –** Soldiers', Airmen's Scripture Readers Association
- **SAPPERS –** Combat engineer
- **SA 80 –** Small Arms for the 1980s, British family of 5.56mm small arms
- **SME –** subject matter expert
- **SOP –** Standard Operating Procedures
- **STAND TO –** part of a command given in drill ('stand to arms')
- **THEATRE –** term used to describe location of a military operation
- **TOUR –** a military job or posting lasting usually two to three years
- **TPT –** tracer projectile round
- **UNPROFOR –** Inited Nations Protection Force
- **WARDROOM –** naval mess
- **WIS –** wounded, injured or sick soldiers
- **XO –** Executive Officer or Second in Command (a naval position)

The Armed Forces' Christian Union (AFCU)

AFCU

Prayerfully serving those who serve

The AFCU is one of a number of British Military Christian organisations. It is an all-ranks, tri-Service organisation of Christians who wish to grow in their faith and share it with those around them.

Prayer:

Undergirding everything we do is prayer. A key part of this is that serving members are offered the dedicated consistent prayer support of a group of associate members who pray for them in strict confidence. There are also Bible study or prayer groups running in or near military bases around the world. As a member you will receive information on where and when to find these groups.

In Touch:

We seek to put members in touch with one another worldwide, especially on posting. Our address list is published in the members-only area of the website and updated regularly.

Literature:

We produce a magazine called *Contact*, teaching material, Bible reading notes and newsletters for members. Mailings are sent out by email every three months.

Events:

We offer skiing, sailing, family and teenagers' holidays, teaching and equipping weekends, ladies' events and day conferences and marriage courses.

Anyone can join! The only condition for membership is belief in prayer to God through our Lord Jesus Christ and a willingness to pray for the spiritual welfare of the Armed Forces. Whether you are a student heading for the Services, a serving member of HM Forces, a retired serviceman or woman or none of these, you are very welcome!

How to join the AFCU:

Either write to or email the AFCU office:
The Armed Forces' Christian Union, Havelock House,
Barrack Road, Aldershot, Hampshire, GU11 3NP
Email: **office@afcu.org.uk**
Tel: 01252 311221

Or visit our website and join online at: **www.afcu.org.uk**

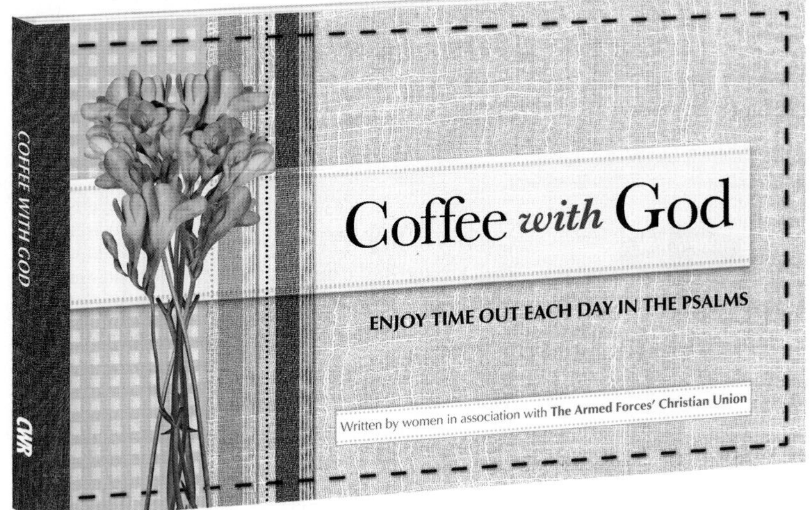
COFFEE WITH GOD
CWR
Coffee with God
ENJOY TIME OUT EACH DAY IN THE PSALMS
Written by women in association with The Armed Forces' Christian Union